THE
THEORY OF EDUCATION
IN
PLATO'S REPUBLIC

THE
THEORY OF EDUCATION
IN
PLATO'S REPUBLIC

By
R. L. NETTLESHIP

With an Introduction
by
SPENCER LEESON

OXFORD UNIVERSITY PRESS
LONDON : HUMPHREY MILFORD

OXFORD
UNIVERSITY PRESS
AMEN HOUSE, E.C. 4
London Edinburgh Glasgow
New York Toronto Melbourne
Capetown Bombay Calcutta
Madras Shanghai
HUMPHREY MILFORD
PUBLISHER TO THE
UNIVERSITY

FIRST EDITION 1935

Reprinted photographically in Great Britain in 1939
by LOWE & BRYDONE, PRINTERS, LTD., LONDON, from
sheets of the first edition

INTRODUCTION

THE Essay that is here reprinted was first published in *Hellenica* in 1880. Its author, Richard Lewis Nettleship, was born in 1846, and from 1869 till his death in the Alps in 1892 he was a Fellow and Tutor in Philosophy at Balliol College, Oxford. Pupils of his who survive speak of his extraordinary power as a teacher, and especially as an expounder of Plato. Except for this Essay and a Memoir of T. H. Green he published nothing; but after his death some of his philosophical lectures and remains were brought together and issued in two volumes, one of which contains his lectures on Plato's *Republic*.

Much has been written about the educational sections of the *Republic*, but so far as I know there is no publication in English other than this Essay which treats Plato's views on education as a single whole, with fullness and yet within a manageable compass. Moreover the merits of the Essay are in themselves very great, and no teacher could wish for any better introduction to the study and practice of his calling. The theory of education, like the theory of so much else, begins with Plato, and some knowledge of what he thought upon that subject has for a long time been required in those who follow courses in Education in Universities and Training Colleges. But up to now those who knew of Nettleship's Essay have had to go to *Hellenica*, and *Hellenica* is difficult to get hold of. All of us therefore who are eager to investigate the philosophical assumptions and beliefs by which our daily work is directed will feel grateful to the Oxford University Press for reprinting and republishing the Essay in separate form, to Messrs. Longmans, Green & Co. and to Nettleship's literary executors for their courtesy in permitting the work to be undertaken, and to the Trustees of the Jowett Copyright Fund, who have generously contributed towards the expenses of printing.

The text has been taken from the second edition of *Hellenica*, published in 1898. The four section headings and the marginal notes are not to be found there; they have been introduced into this edition in order that the progress of the argument may be more easily grasped by readers who do not know the *Republic* in the original.

There was probably never a time when more thought and care was given than it is to-day to working out the best methods of teaching particular subjects, and to all that concerns the organization and material equipment of the Schools. But there is much dissension and confusion upon what is the supreme purpose, or the 'architectonic end', for the attainment of which all the rest exists; and it is useless, as well as illogical, to consider schemes of organization and methods of instruction until we have set before ourselves a clear idea of this ultimate objective. Such and such a scheme or method is best; but best for

what? passing examinations, or 'getting on', or training in citizenship, or the development of personality,
or what? This primary question needs thinking out.

Plato calls us back to first questions and first principles. His purpose is to foster the growth of the
human soul towards the good; and true again to the
logical order, he does not attempt to suggest methods
of achieving this end until he has subjected the soul
to an analysis, so that the teacher may know what it is
that he is set to treat before he begins to think how he
shall treat it. I am not here concerned, nor am I
qualified, to consider whether Plato's aim is the true
aim, nor whether his analysis of the soul is accurate
or complete, nor whether the methods he suggests for
training the soul towards that end are sound. The
value of the Essay for us is that it may convict us of sin
in respect of our muddled thinking about aims and
methods and means and ends. We may watch a great
mind working upon a great subject, in all its length
and breadth and height and depth. As always he
asks, not necessarily for our assent, but for a resolute
effort to clear our minds of hazy half-truths and windy
phrases and to think the whole matter out again from
the beginning, bringing the means into relation with
the end.

Even for those who know the *Republic* it would be
a hard task to collect for themselves from all parts of
the dialogue the thoughts about education that Plato
has scattered up and down the work. Nettleship does
this for us in a masterly way. Moreover, his Essay is

not simply an analysis, but in itself a living whole; and the currents of English thought about education have not moved so far since 1880 as to render his general reflections out of date.

SPENCER LEESON

April 1935.

I. INTRODUCTION: THE INDIVIDUAL AND SOCIETY

SOME apology may seem to be due for printing an Essay upon a subject so well worn as the Platonic conception of Education, the more so as I have no new discoveries to detail and no new theories to advance. But it seems true that Greek thought is in a sense ever young; that while its lessons are always being learnt, they are always being forgotten and misunderstood; and that though much has been done for its interpretation, and the study of it has established itself in the curriculum of our schools and Universities, we are still in many respects only at the threshold, and often see it through a veil of conventional platitudes, pretentious antiquarianism, or sentimental finery. All that I have here attempted is to draw renewed attention to some of the salient and familiar points in a subject which concerns us all, and to suggest reflection upon our own corresponding theory and practice.

The subject of Education is treated by Plato in the *Republic* as an integral and vital part of the wider subject of the well-being of human society, and it is scarcely possible to give an intelligent account of his treatment without first indicating the scope and plan of the work as a whole. The *Republic* opens by asking the question, What is the nature of justice? and the first four books of it pursue the answer to this question without any serious deviation. The real bearing of the question is but poorly represented to us in its

What is the Good Life?

English dress; it would be better expressed, if (following the suggestion of Plato himself) we substituted for
it the question, How are men to order their lives so
as to live best? which naturally involves the further
question, What is to live well? Various representative
answers to these questions are first propounded and
examined; the personal experience of the good old
man of the good old time, the half-understood maxims
of the educated man of the world, the sounding formulas of the unscrupulous and cynical rhetorician—
all these are passed in review, and found to be inadequate, ill-considered, or self-destructive. Then the
voice of society or its leaders is listened to; current
theories of the origin of the law and morality, which
resolve the one into arbitrary convention and the
other into a calculation of rewards and punishments,
or a system of indulgences, are exhibited in their
most naked form; until at last we seem to be left with
the whole of popular opinion and experience arrayed
upon the side of what is called injustice, and upon the
other side nothing but a bare conviction, to which
the moral sense of man still clings, though unable to
justify itself for doing so.

The ques-
tion can
best be
answered
by an ana-
lysis of
human
society and
the human
soul

Such a justification Socrates is now called upon to
give. We have had enough of verbal discussions in
which everything seems to depend upon the sense in
which the particular disputant takes the particular
word in dispute; nor can we rest satisfied with theories
which reduce morality to its material consequences,
whether in this world or the next. If justice and
injustice, right and wrong, are not merely the same

thing viewed from different sides, but express real and radical distinctions, they must admit of being exhibited 'as they are in themselves', that is, not in their current equivalents of wealth, success, popularity, and the reverse, but as forces working for good or ill in the very soul of man. With the demand for such an exhibition, the inquiry passes from the domain of verbal definition and popular opinion to that of psychology, and the question, How are we to order our lives for the best? becomes the question, What is the nature of the living principle within us which Plato calls the soul? Though, however, this is the real import of the transition now made in the dialogue, it is made in a form which would be little expected by a modern student of moral psychology. Instead of meeting the new requirement by analysing the human soul, Plato proceeds to analyse human society. The reason for this is to be found in his conviction that in society (to interpret his own familiar simile) we see man 'writ large'; in other words, that in the broad outlines of the state, with its classes, its trade and industry, its military and political institutions, the secret and subtle elements of human nature come to the surface, take visible shape, and are unmistakably legible to the observer. If then we would study human life successfully, we must begin from the outside and work inwards; we must take the obvious facts and principles without which society would not go on, and ask, what they mean, of what inner facts and principles are they the exponents? And in order to do this, we must have a method. It will not do to take society at any chance point on its surface and probe it there; we must begin at the beginning, we must look at it 'in its growth'. Not, however, in its historical, but in its logical and psychological 'growth'; for this seems to be the explanation of the picture which Plato gives of 'the genesis of the State'. He has begun with what he considered the lowest stratum of life, at the point where it is most nearly the mere keeping life alive, the mere satisfaction of necessary wants; to this rudimentary basis he has gradually added the higher factors of human nature, with their accompanying needs; and throughout the structure, alike in its lower and its higher ranges, he has shown us the same principle of efficiency and well-being, a principle writ large on the face of society, but to be ultimately traced back to its analogue in the constitution of the human soul itself. That principle, to which he gives the name of justice, may be briefly explained as follows:—Every man has wants, of which he cannot get rid, but which he cannot himself satisfy. They are as various as the want of food and clothes, the want of protection from external violence, the want of assistance against his own lower nature; but whatever their character, they make him individually insufficient for himself. On the other hand, while all men need others, all men are, or may be, needed by others; the same limitation which forces the individual into society also makes him a useful member of it; for the diversity of individual character is not a mere diversity of atoms, but has in it the capability of organization, or, in other words, of forming a whole. These primary facts suggest, as the true principle of human life, that each social element should do that which it is most fitted to do, thus contributing to the common stock the best that it has to give, and receiving from each other element that of which it is itself most in need. The more society is so ordered that this twofold principle of division and association of work is carried out, the more nearly will it approach its most natural and most perfect form. The main part of the first section of the *Republic*, from the middle of the second to the end of the fourth book, is occupied with the sketch of a society as it might be conceived to be if this principle of harmonious co-operation were realized, and it is as an element in its realization that what may be called the first system of education is developed.

Education as an element in the realization of a perfect society

II. THE NATURE OF THE SOUL

BEFORE considering that system in its details, it will be well to see what was Plato's conception of education in general, for by it his whole treatment of the subject is in a great measure determined. We know in our own time what a difference it may make in the spirit and working of an educational method, whether the idea with which it starts is that of culture, or of training, or of useful accomplishment. Plato's idea of the essence of education is most simply and comprehensively expressed in the word 'nurture'. To him the human soul is emphatically and before all else something living, something which in the strict sense we can neither create nor destroy, but which we can feed or starve, nourish or poison. As in the case

'Nurture' the essence of Education

of other living things, of plants and animals, the stronger and better the nature of the soul, the more important is it what nourishment it gets, and a gifted soul in a corrupt society is like a good seed sown in a strange soil; it grows crooked and unlike itself, loses its proper virtue, and sinks at last to the level of its surroundings. And in another famous passage, to which we shall have to refer more than once, the young citizen who is being educated is compared to an animal at pasture; from the things which he sees and hears about him he assimilates, little by little, the good or the evil which they embody, till 'many a little makes a mickle', which becomes part and parcel of himself. It is this feeling of the assimilative power of the soul which leads Plato to attach such immense importance to the circumstances and environment of life, and makes him on the whole more disposed to attribute moral evil to bad nurture than to inherent vice. Amongst the various elements which make up the complex creature man, he conceives that there are few which are not open to good influence. Of what are usually called the lower desires there are indeed some that are radically 'wild', and with these there is only one course possible, to stop their growth; but the others admit of being 'tamed', and made to take service under the higher self. And thus it is with a sort of compassion that Plato looks upon some of the great criminals of the world, who in his eyes had the capability of being its greatest benefactors, and owe their failure to its corruption or neglect. Against the all-powerful influence of society, he thinks that no

[marginal note:] The growth of the soul and its power of assimilating good and evil

private teaching can hold its ground. It is not the so-called enlightened leaders of public opinion, the sophists of the day, who really teach and demoralize the youth; the real educator and the real sophist is public opinion itself, whose voice, resounding in the assembly and the law courts, in the theatre and the camp, is practically irresistible by the isolated efforts of individuals. Such a power for evil can only be counteracted by creating a power for good as penetrating, as unconscious, and as universal, and to do this is the true function of a public system of education. On the other hand, while the inherent vitality of the soul makes the question of its nourishment all-important, it also precludes a merely mechanical treatment of it. We can place it in a healthy atmosphere, but we cannot compel it to assimilate only the healthy elements. The 'eye of the soul' is not, as some 'professors of education' seem to think, a blind eye into which knowledge can be put; its power of vision can neither be originally produced by education, nor entirely destroyed by the want of it; it can only be 'turned to the light', for which it has an intrinsic capacity. And the same holds good of the lower extremity of human nature; as in the 'wild' and unteachable element there is a power of growth which can only be dealt with by being repressed, so among men there are found moral 'incurables', for whom society has no course but to put them out of the way.

The very simplicity of these ideas, as in the case of some others of Plato, is apt to conceal their importance. Everybody admits in theory that the human self is a living being, requiring a certain environment in order to grow properly, and capable of growing improperly in an immense variety of ways. But it is mainly in dealing with the material circumstances of life that the truth of the principle is practically realized, because there the consequences of its neglect are palpable: when we have to do with the mental atmosphere we are liable to forget it. Then again, the greater specialization of modern life makes it difficult for us to keep our hold on universal elementary truths, which to the Greeks seemed neither old nor simple. Modern education inevitably divides itself under many heads; it is primary or higher, technical or liberal, scientific or religious; the distinctions are real and cannot be ignored; but in the controversies to which they sometimes give rise it is well, just because it is hard, to remember, that the ultimate subject of all education is a living organism, whose vital power, though divisible in thought, is really one and undivided; that its vital wants are equally such, whether they be for fresh air, for useful knowledge, or for religious truth; and that it will starve or degenerate in mind if its natural mental nourishment be denied it, as surely as it will in body if its bodily wants be neglected.

The growing soul needs its own proper nurture

Such being Plato's general conception of the nature of education, we may expect that any system of education which he propounds will be a system for providing proper nurture to the growing soul, or for adjusting its surroundings to its higher needs. It is also clear that the particular character of the system for attaining these ends must be determined by the conception of the human nature which has to be fed, and the needs to which its circumstances have to be adjusted. And thus, in order to understand Plato's theory of education, we must understand his psychology.

In giving some account of the psychology of the *Republic*, we shall have to notice that, while the groundplan of the account of the soul remains on the whole the same, the position assigned to its various elements changes considerably in different parts of the work; and these changes are necessarily accompanied by changes in the view taken of education. We will begin with the psychology of the first section of the work, only combining that of later sections where it seems to be in substantial agreement. From this we gather that Plato regarded the human soul as a complex whole, consisting of three 'forms', 'kinds', or 'parts', as he variously calls them. The first of these, beginning at the lower end in the scale of worth, is ἐπιθυμία or 'appetite'. Plato was aware that in what he called the 'appetitive' form of the soul he was dealing with something too various to be easily described by a single name. He seems to have chosen the name in question because the bodily appetites, to which it was commonly appropriated, are, from their intensity, the most obvious and conspicuous instances of their class. He has, however, another name, suggested, not by the degree of intensity of the activity, but by what seemed to him its most typical object; 'because wealth is the principal instrument by which the bodily appetites are satisfied, we call this element of the soul

But first we must consider the nature of the soul

It consists of three parts: first, 'appetite'

the wealth-loving or gain-loving element'. This close
association of things sometimes supposed to be so far
apart as sensuality and avarice, is very characteristic
of Plato; and we shall see later on by what facts he
illustrates it. For the present it is enough to observe
that, though Plato by no means confines the word
translated 'appetite' to the above-mentioned instances,
yet when he speaks of the 'appetitive' as a specific
form or part of the soul, he intends primarily those
desires of which bodily satisfaction and wealth are
the typical objects. Of such appetites he distinguishes
in a later book two kinds, 'necessary' and 'unnecessary'. Necessary appetites are those which we cannot
get rid of, or those of which the satisfaction does us
good; unnecessary are those which are superfluous
or harmful. In these latter, again, there is a sub-
division into those which, though in themselves unproductive and wasteful to the organism, are yet
capable of regulation, and those which are incurably
'wild', 'bestial', 'lawless', which make themselves felt,
even in the best of men, when reason is in abeyance,
but which, unless repressed or reduced to a minimum,
bring ruin into life. These distinctions are graphically
reproduced in a somewhat generalized form in one of
the allegorical figures under which Plato represents
his conception of human nature. He asks us to imagine
a being having the outward semblance of a man, but
combining within three creatures, a man, a lion, and
'a beast with many heads, heads of beasts tame and
wild, and able to breed and change them at its will'.
Of the first two there will be more to say presently;

in the third we readily recognize the psychological element of appetite in the sense just described. The hydra-like creature has in it an inherent capacity of growth and reproduction; some of its offspring can be 'tamed' and 'domesticated', and made serviceable to life; others are radically untameable, the inorganic, inhuman, 'unnecessary,' and possibly destructive, appendage of our nature, which, while it can never entirely divest itself of its humanity, touches God at one extremity and the beast at the other.

Though Plato represents appetite as the element which occupies the largest space in the soul, and though the men who live for appetite more than for any other part of themselves are, in his view, the majority of mankind, we shall not expect it to occupy the chief share of attention in his system of education. The degree of education of which the appetites are capable is expressed by his own word 'taming', and by this he seems to mean such a regulation of them as shall prevent them from interfering with the higher psychical activities, and train them to contribute to the good of the whole soul that basis of healthy physical life which is the necessary groundwork of those activities.

which we must tame

The second element in the Platonic analysis of the soul is not quite so easily described or understood. The Greek words θυμός, τὸ θυμοειδές, by which it is designated, are commonly translated 'spirit', and though this term covers only a part of their meaning in the *Republic*, it will serve as well as any other in the absence of a real equivalent. 'Spirit' is first introduced

Second, 'spirit'

as being the indispensable foundation of courage, that element of hardihood and intrepidity which is common to men with dogs and horses, and which makes them 'never say die'; at the same time it is represented as the source of pugnacity and aggressiveness, with their possible developments into ferocity and cruelty. It is only another form of the same view, when 'spirit' is said to be that part of the soul which is peculiarly fostered and stimulated by athletic exercises; it is the 'hard' element in human nature, which, if rightly nurtured, becomes true bravery, but if exclusively encouraged degenerates into blind brutality, surliness, quarrelsomeness, or self-will. In all this we at once recognize the 'lion' of the allegorical figure of man mentioned above.

So far the account of the 'spirited' element is simple enough. It has two other senses which are not quite so obvious; the one attaching to the sense of anger which θυμός so commonly has, the other to that of pugnacity. From the former point of view 'spirit' appears as what we may call righteous indignation. It is that which makes a man's blood boil at the consciousness of suffering unjustly, while it is characteristically absent when the suffering is felt to be deserved. It is that, again, which makes a man angry with himself when he feels that he has let his appetites get the better of his reason, whereas no one ever feels this anger when he has let his better judgement prevail over his appetite. These observations lead Plato to represent 'spirit' as the natural ally or servant of the rational or better self; not that it is never irrational, or

Forms in which this manifests itself, for good or evil

may not be perverted by bad education, but that it never seems to act with the lower appetites against the reason; or, to use more modern phraseology, if we are once convinced that in refusing to satisfy an appetite we are acting reasonably, we may feel dissatisfaction, but we do not feel indignation. In its third and last distinctive use, 'spirit is the root of ambition or the competitive instinct. In this sense it is, as was said, a modification of the fighting spirit, for the essence both of ambition and of pugnacity is the desire to do better than somebody else. And as in the other two senses, so here 'spirit' may have a good or a bad development, into honourable rivalry on the one hand, on the other into mere contentiousness.

It is not difficult to see how these various representations of 'spirit' may be connected. In all of them there is an element of what we may call self-assertion and self-consciousness. It is this, in the form of not choosing to be 'put upon', which makes us resist what we think injustice; it is this, in the form of honourable pride, which makes us face danger without flinching, and prompts us to measure ourselves against others; it is the consciousness of a self which deserves respect that makes us angry when we have disgraced ourselves; and it is the feeling that there is no such self to fall back upon which weakens us when we know that we are in the wrong; and lastly, it is often an exaggerated sense of our own importance or power which breaks out into aggressiveness, hardens into self-will, or is nursed into bad temper.

It now remains to consider the third, and in Plato's Third,

mind the highest, element in the constitution of the
'the philo- human soul, that which he calls 'the philosophic'.
sophic' And here much more than in the case of the other two
we shall have to notice considerable modifications in
his account in different parts of the *Republic*.

Beginning with what we have called the first main
section of the work, we find the 'philosophic' element
at first characterized in a way very far removed from
what the English word would lead us to expect. It
is introduced as a necessary psychological comple-
ment to the element of 'spirit'. Unmitigated or
unbalanced, the latter element would be a source of
mere indiscriminate pugnacity, and would result in
a destructive war of all against all. Clearly if human
nature is to be adapted to the higher functions of civic
society, it must contain some counterbalancing factor,
some quality of gentleness to soften ferocity, some
tendency to union to counteract the feeling of mutual
antagonism. The germs of such an element Plato
finds in some of the lower animals: the well-bred dog,
who had been already chosen to typify the quality of
'spirit', is found to exhibit, along with the greatest
fierceness towards strangers, the greatest gentleness
towards those whom he knows; and this suggests,
what is found to be the fact when we come to look at
human nature, that this combination of qualities so
opposite is not only possible but natural. But the
question arises, Why call this softening, unifying element 'philosophic'? Here again, half-playfully perhaps, yet not without a deeper meaning, Plato helps
himself with the analogy of the dog. The dog judges

of friends and enemies by the test of knowledge; those whom he knows he treats as friends, those whom he does not know as enemies; with him, in a word, to know is to be fond; and as it is the feeling of knowing those whom he knows which excites his fondness, he may be said in a sense to be fond of knowing, much as a person who likes the society of his inferiors might be said to be fond of superiority. In so far then as the quality of gentleness attaches to the consciousness of knowledge and the pleasure which that consciousness excites, it may be said to arise from fondness of knowledge, and this is almost equivalent to 'philosophy' in its literal sense of 'love of knowledge' or 'wisdom'.

The first and simplest application of this somewhat curious train of thought is obvious enough. Every one has felt in one form or another the power of knowledge or familiarity to breed a sort of liking. It is an instinctive feeling, which often does not rise to the height of affection, but remains a sense of quiet pleasure or comfort; it attaches to things, to places, to persons; much of the love of home and of country, and even of humanity, is traceable to its presence; much of the antipathy to foreigners or to novelties, to its absence. In such a rudimentary feeling of attachment for what belongs to us Plato saw the first germ of that which seemed to him highest in human nature. We shall see shortly how the germ developed under his hands.

Our next introduction to the 'philosophic' element of the soul is in a somewhat different context. It is still, indeed, the 'gentle' or 'tame' part in contradistinction to the 'wildness' and 'hardness' of the 'spirited part', and it is still intimately associated with knowledge; but the gentleness of which it is now said to be the source is the result of culture instead of dog-like attachment, and the knowledge in which it takes delight is the sense of something understood rather than of something familiar. It now includes suscepti-bility to the influences of language, of music, of painting, of beauty in the widest sense of the word; it includes also the quickness of perception which makes learning pleasant and welcomes every fresh form of truth. It has also a more purely moral aspect; it is that which produces love of order and quietness, the impulse to obey rather than to resist, and to use persuasion rather than force. Like 'spirit', it is capable of exaggeration and perversion; under the exclusive or excessive influence of culture and refine-ment it develops softness and effeminacy, or nervous sensibility and unstableness.

This in different forms and under different names is the ruling element

When we again meet with the highest form of the soul it is no longer under the name of 'philosophic'; the intellectual character in it now predominates over the emotional; it is the calculative, deliberative, reasoning element in the soul, that in virtue of which it guides and rules, that which when fully developed becomes, not love of wisdom, but wisdom. Its relation to the 'spirited' element is also changed; from being a merely complementary factor to it, it has come to be its natural master, from whom issue the dogmas and principles which in the well-trained soul 'appe-tite' cheerfully obeys and 'spirit' fearlessly carries out.

Such is the account of the 'philosophic' part in the

first section of the *Republic*; in its most primitive
character it is the impulse of attraction to what is
familiar because it is familiar; then the substratum of
gentleness and of culture; lastly, reason in its regu-
lative and ruling capacity.

To sum up then briefly the results thus far arrived
at, the human soul, in Plato's view, is a triple being.
It has for its largest constituent appetite, the simple
craving for present satisfaction, capable of indefinite
expansion, mostly amenable, but also partially un-
amenable, to reason. Secondly, it implies an element of self-assertiveness and pugnacity, which gives
rise to qualities as various as courage and brutality,
ambition and contentiousness, just indignation and
unreasoning bad temper. Lastly, there is in it a capacity of attraction and receptivity, which if not perverted into weakness of character, develops, on the
one side, into gentleness, sociableness, love; on the
other, into refinement, culture, and wisdom.

Proceeding now to the later modifications of this
psychology, we find, as has been already observed,
that they are modifications not so much in the general
constitution of the soul as in the relationship of its
constituent elements. They consist mainly in the
widening and deepening of the conception of the
'philosophic element', and in the assignment to it of
a much more predominant position in the formation
of human character and the regulation of human
conduct. It is scarcely possible to make this clear
without again referring shortly to the general structure of the *Republic*. The first four books of it, as we

Deeper
meaning
attached to
'the philo-
sophic' as
an element
in the soul

saw, contain the discovery and exhibition of a principle of human life, social and individual, such as, if carried out, would realize the greatest well-being of which man is capable. That principle is most simply described as the harmonious co-operation of various elements, whether those of the individual soul or those of the state; and the ultimate hypothesis upon which the principle rests is that these various elements have the capacity of forming a whole, and that therefore, in performing each their separate function in the best way, they are also in the best way working for the good of the whole. According to this view, in a normally constituted society each class would consist of those individuals in whom a certain psychological quality predominated, and who were therefore best fitted for a certain kind of work; and the chief interest and duty of the society would be to secure, firstly, that each of its members should have his proper place in the organization of work; and, secondly, that having found his proper place, he should be fitted by education or other means to do the particular work of his life as well as possible. Of the work necessary to the well-being of a state, Plato thought that there were three principal kinds, the work of producing the material commodities essential to life, the work of protecting the state against external enemies and of preserving order within it, and the work of legislation and government. For the class of citizens engaged in the first kind of work he apparently did not think that any public system of education was necessary, a fact which, however much at variance with modern ideas, will not startle any one who is familiar with the position of the industrial classes in Greek society, and with the opinions entertained of them both by the public and by philosophers. It was then for the classes who are engaged in military and political functions, that is, in what a Greek would consider the functions of a citizen proper, that the education sketched in the earlier part of the *Republic* is exclusively intended. That education is a method for providing the natural and proper nurture for the souls of the persons in question. Its character (to anticipate for a moment what must be said later) is emphatically non-technical; it teaches no knowledge or mental accomplishment having a direct bearing upon the functions eventually to be exercised by those who receive it; it comes to an end at about twenty, when those functions have not yet begun, and its main object is to predispose the soul, intellectually and morally, to the perception and execution of ideas and principles of which it does not as yet understand the full bearing, but upon which it will afterwards find that the welfare of itself and society depends.

We may now return to the point at which it was necessary to make this digression. It seems to have been in Plato's mind, even at the time when he was writing the first part of the *Republic*, that the system of education contained in it was imperfect and inadequate. Whether it was from design that he deferred the expression of this feeling, or whether it was forced from him by subsequent criticism, this is not the place to discuss; it is at any rate certain that in what may

illustrated from different parts of the work

be called the second section of the work, comprising the fifth, sixth, and seventh books, the education described in the preceding books is referred to and criticized as insufficient for the purpose of preparing citizens for the exercise of the most important public functions. This attitude of criticism adopted in the later towards the earlier section is, however, by no means the only symptom of change on the part of the writer. The question under discussion, the tone in which it is discussed, and the answer which is given to it, are very different in the two parts. In the first the question is, What is the true principle which should regulate human life, and what would be the form of a society in which it was carried out? In the second it is, How could such an ideal society, with all the consequences which it seems logically to entail, be actually realized, and what is the root of the existing evils of mankind which hinder its realization? In the first part, again, the tone is that of a man who certainly sees much to criticize in existing institutions, but who is nevertheless disposed to make the best of them, and does not despair of doing so. In the second it is that of one oppressed by the sense of the evil in the world, hoping for salvation only from remedies which are themselves almost hopeless, diffident and yet defiant, daringly paradoxical and yet terribly in earnest. And lastly, the two answers are different. To the earlier question the answer is: Allow, and if necessary compel, human nature to develop normally, and provide it with the nurture which its development demands; the rest will manage itself. To the later it is: The cause of the ills of mankind is ignorance of their true good and neglect of their noblest natures; train those natures rightly and they will see what is the true good of mankind; give them unlimited power and they will carry out what the good requires. Such is the significance of the startling demand made in the fifth book of the *Republic*, that philosophers should be kings. We are here concerned with it, not in its political, but in its psychological and educational, aspect; in other words, we have to see how Plato's conception of what we have already learnt to know as the 'philosophic part' in the soul has expanded to the point at which we now find it, giving its name to the whole man, embodying all gifts and excellencies, and claiming to rule the world.

Between the account of the 'philosophic' element *and culminating* which we have gathered from the first four books of *in the* the *Republic*, and that of the 'philosophic nature' which *embodiment of all* we are about to gather from the following three, the *specifically human ex-* references made to the same subject in the ninth book *cellencies* seem to occupy an intermediate place, and to form a kind of transition. In the ninth book, taking his departure from the triple division of the soul with which we are now familiar, Plato divides mankind into three 'primary kinds', according as one or other of the three psychical elements predominates in the character. To those in whom 'appetite' predominates, the chief object in life is the wealth by which appetite is satisfied; to the 'spirited' class it is the honour which rewards successful competition; while to those in whom the 'philosophic' side is the strongest, it is truth.

And accordingly they are called respectively lovers of gain or wealth, lovers of contention or honour, lovers of learning or wisdom, that is, 'philosophers', and of these the last are said to enjoy the fullest experience and to live the highest life. Here then we find the love of knowing, which has all along underlain in different senses the 'philosophic' form of soul, interpreted as the love of 'knowing the nature of the truth', or, to use an equivalent Platonic phrase, 'the nature of what is,' and further, when present in sufficient force, giving its name to a definite type of character, and that the highest. The allegorical figure of man in the same book, to which reference has already been made, supplies some more additions to the conception. In the triple creature which we are there asked to imagine, the 'man', or, as he is called to distinguish him from the external human semblance, the 'inward man', clearly represents the 'philosophic' element; and from this we see that in Plato's view it is this element which constitutes the real humanity, and there-

the truly human and therefore also the truly divine element in man

fore the real personality, in our complex nature. But this is not all. The 'inward man' is distinctly asserted to be that which is 'divine' or 'the most divine' in man. To Plato there is a revelation of God in the human soul, as there is in the physical world; his 'celestial city' is not only a visionary type, it is also, like the 'kingdom of heaven', within us, and he who will may enter in and dwell there. And once more, as it is this divine humanity which is in the truest sense the self, the other parts of human nature are conceived by Plato to find their highest activity and their most real satisfaction in following and serving it as far as they are able; to become as human as possible, to live for humanity in this sense, is the highest end of the half-animal nature which forms the larger part of man.

Turning now from the ninth to the three central books of the *Republic*, we find the attributes with which the 'philosophic' nature is invested in the former confirmed and developed in the latter. The point of departure is the same: the 'philosopher' is described, in accordance with his name, as one who loves knowledge or wisdom, and 'philosophy' is the instinctive and indiscriminate craving to learn. The man endowed with this passion is like a man with a great appetite and a strong digestion; everything that will stay the hunger of his soul is welcome food. Or again, he is like a man who is in love, not once or twice, but always and everywhere; as the lover finds nothing that is not beautiful in the face of his beloved, so to the man born to be a 'philosopher' there is nothing in the face of truth which is not lovable. This is the germ, the elementary condition, of philosophy; it does not of itself make a full-grown philosopher, any more than the possession of 'spirit' necessarily makes a brave man; but no true philosopher can be without it, any more than a spiritless man can have real courage. But (and here Plato takes his next great step) these elementary qualities are not only the germ of the true philosophic character, but of all human excellence as well; or rather, the philosophic spirit cannot exist in its fullness and integrity without involving all that

[marginal notes:] The passion for knowledge

the love of the beautiful

is called good and noble in human character. Plato
explains this somewhat startling idea by showing how
the whole company of virtues flows naturally and
necessarily from the single passion for truth. In one
whose desires 'set strongly' towards one all-absorb-
ing object, the channels of the bodily appetites must
run dry; and the 'vision of all time and all existence'
which he enjoys will make human life seem but a
little thing, and death nothing to be feared. In a
mind which 'reaches out after all that is human and
divine' there is no room for meanness or pettiness,
nor can such a mind be harsh or unfair in dealings
with other men, for the motives which make others
so—avarice, conceit, or fear—do not touch it. Add to
these ethical qualities the intellectual gifts without
which love of knowledge is impossible, quickness to
learn and slowness to forget, with that mental grace
or proportion which predisposes the soul to receive
truth, and we have a fully endowed nature, such as
'the god of blame himself could find no fault in'.

quickness of apprehension, grace and proportion of soul

We have here reached the culminating point in the
development of Plato's conception of 'philosophy' in
the *Republic*. Beginning with the instinctive attraction
to what is familiar, passing on into the ready receptivity for all that is admirable in nature and art, with
the unconscious grace and refinement which accom-
panies it, it has now become the consuming passion
for what is true and real, at once the most human and
the most divine attribute of the soul, the crowning
gift and complete embodiment of perfect manhood.

in a word Perfect Manhood

Neither the later uses of the word 'philosophy', nor

its literal interpretation as 'love of wisdom', will much help the modern reader to enter here into the spirit of Plato. Philosophy to most of us is too much wrapt up in the associations of books and systems, of technicalities and jargon, to let us feel the living spirit which it still is when it is anything more than a set of phrases. And the love of truth, in spite of the boasts of modern science, is still but rarely found to dominate the character and mould the life as Plato conceived that it might do. The difficulty of understanding him is further increased by the dispersion and differentiation which his idea has undergone. When he spoke of 'the truth', or of 'what is', we see that there entered into his feeling not only the enthusiasm of the scientific discoverer, but also the passion of the poet for beauty and the devotion of the saint to the object of his worship. It would be beyond our present scope to dwell at length upon this point; a reference to two passages in the *Republic* will sufficiently illustrate it. One is that in which he describes the philosophic spirit as the desire for union of the mind with reality: 'It is in the nature of the real lover of learning to be ever struggling up to being, and not to abide amongst the manifold and limited objects of opinion; he will go on his way, and the edge of his love will not grow dull nor its force abate, until he has got hold of the nature of being with that part of his soul to which it belongs so to do, and that is the part which is akin to being; with this he will draw near, and mingle being with being, and beget intelligence and truth, and find knowledge and true life and nourishment, and then, and not till then, he will cease from his travail.' The imagery of this passage shows us that to Plato the process of knowledge was very far from being the mechanical and external operation as which we are apt to regard it. To him the world of reality or fact, that which really is in spite of what appears or what we fancy, is something of kindred nature with what is highest in the human mind; the impulse to know is the impulse to become one with that which is 'bone of our bone and flesh of our flesh', and truth is the birth which allays the 'travail of the soul'.

In another passage the effect of the same spirit upon the formation of character is brought out in a way equally remote from ordinary modes of thought. 'The man whose mind is really set upon the things that are, has not leisure to look down at the concerns of men, and to fight with them, and fill himself with envy and bitterness; that which he sees and gazes upon is set fast and ever the same, it neither does nor suffers wrong, but is all reasonable and in order. This he imitates, and, as far as possible, becomes like it, for it surely cannot be that a man can live in fellowship with what he admires without imitating it. So then the philosopher, living in fellowship with what is divine and orderly, grows himself orderly and divine as far as man is able.' Such is Plato's conception of what in modern phrase we should call the genuine study of the laws of nature and the world. In the unchangeable order and beauty of the universe he sees the image on a vaster scale of the same reason which is imperfectly reflected in human life, and he might have said to Justice what Wordsworth has said to Duty:

> 'Thou dost preserve the stars from wrong,
> And the most ancient heavens through thee are fresh and strong.'

We have now passed in review the main elements of that human nature for which, as Plato conceived, it was the function of education to provide nurture. It may seem, perhaps, that a disproportionate space has been given to what belongs not to education but to psychology. But it is just the inseparableness of the two that is so characteristic of Plato's treatment, and, whatever we may think of his analysis of the soul in its details, we shall hardly escape the conclusion that some such analysis is an indispensable condition of a really rational theory of education; in other words, that neither a state nor an individual can undertake to educate in a systematic way unless they start with some idea, not only of what they wish to teach, nor only of the type of character which they wish to produce, but also of the living being to which the matter to be taught is relative, and upon which the given character is to be impressed. The 'practical' man, who believes in 'results', will be disposed to regard such psychological considerations as fanciful or far-fetched. And yet the most fatally unpractical thing in the world is to go on testing methods by results which take every factor into account except the one upon which the whole result ultimately depends. That factor in man is the human mind, in Englishmen the English mind, in different classes of Englishmen the minds of those

Necessity of psychological analysis as the basis of any sound system of education classes; and to discuss what kinds of education are in themselves the best, without considering mental organization, is as idle as to discuss what is the best kind of food in the abstract without regard to the stomach which has to digest it.

Before passing on to our main subject, the methods by which Plato proposed to meet the educational needs of the soul, one preliminary observation must be made. It appears from what has been already said that there is a certain want of continuity in his psychology. Instead of following the soul in an unbroken series from its earliest to its most advanced phase of development, he has first given a picture of its education up to a certain point, which is apparently meant to be final, and has then made a fresh start, and represented the previous course as a merely preliminary stage in a larger and more elaborate system; and this fresh start coincides with a fresh point of departure in the account of the highest or 'philosophic' element in the soul. The questions suggested by these facts as to the composition of the *Republic* do not concern us now; whatever they may be, and however they may be answered, it may be assumed here that Plato, at some time in his life, intended the sections of the *Republic*, as we now have it, to form parts of one work. On this assumption, the accounts which it contains both of the soul and of education have been considered in this Essay as forming a logical if not a literary whole, and as supplying a fairly complete and coherent representation of what Plato conceived human nature in its fullness to be and to require. It must, however, be remembered once for all that the *Republic* gives us, not a detailed treatise on education, but certain leading principles which admit of being applied under various circumstances and in various ways. Our present object is not primarily to discover the modifications which these principles admit or require, but to exhibit the principles themselves in their clearest light and fullest bearings.

III. THE ELEMENTARY STAGES: MUSIC AND GYMNASTIC

THE education of the average Greek gentleman, like that of the average English gentleman, comprised a certain amount of mental cultivation and a certain amount of athletic exercise. The former, besides reading, writing, and some elementary mathematics, consisted mainly in the reciting and learning by heart of poetry, along with the elements of music, and sometimes of drawing. Perhaps because so much of the poetry was originally sung or accompanied, the word 'music' was sometimes applied to the education in literature as well as in music proper, and it is in this wider sense that Plato habitually uses it. Under the term 'gymnastic' was understood the whole system of diet and exercise which, varying with the customs of different states, had for its common object the production of bodily health and strength, and the preparation for military service. In this twofold method of education, which the wisdom of the past had handed down, Plato sees an unconscious recog-

Meaning of 'Music' and 'Gymnastic'

1392

nition of the psychological requirements of human nature on its two most important sides. At first sight it would seem that 'music' and 'gymnastic' were related to one another as mental to bodily training, and this was no doubt the ordinary way of distinguishing them; but Plato, while himself adopting the popular phraseology at first, afterwards corrects it by asserting that the soul, and not the body, is the primary object of 'gymnastic' as well as of 'music', and appeals to the fact that exclusive devotion to physical exercises affects the character no less markedly than exclusive devotion to literary and aesthetic culture. The truth is, that 'music' educates, not the soul merely, but specifically the 'philosophic' part of the soul, through the medium of the eye and ear, while 'gymnastic', through bodily exercises, not only produces bodily health and strength, but disciplines the psychological element of 'spirit'. It is through the gentle, responsive, loving element that the soul is open to the influences of literature and art; it is this which makes it quick to assimilate, ready to obey and to imitate, open-eyed and open-eared to catch the sights and sounds of the living world. To satisfy its cravings with the right food, to offer true nobility to its admiration and true beauty to its love, to keep its perceptions wakeful and clear, to refine and balance its emotions, these are, in Plato's opinion, the functions of 'musical' education. But it will not be truly 'musical', truly 'harmonious', unless it be counterbalanced by something different. If the 'philosophic' side of the soul be exclusively fostered, its gentleness will turn into effeminacy, its

The Soul the object of both kinds of training

sensitiveness into irritability, its simple love into feverish desire. It is not enough (though this is important) that the material presented in 'music' should itself be such as to brace the softer qualities in the soul; it must be supplemented by nurture of an altogether different kind acting upon altogether different qualities. This is the office of 'gymnastic', which, by bodily exercises, develops and educates the element of 'spirit'. For 'spirit', though it has an instinctive tendency to ally itself with reason, requires training if the tendency is to become a habit. Proper 'gymnastic' will discipline the wild impulses of violence and pugnacity, developing the intelligent courage of the citizen-soldier, instead of the blind ferocity of the barbarian or the wild beast, while it will counteract the yielding, voluptuous, or nervous tendencies by encouraging competition, endurance, and presence of mind. On the other hand, excessive attention to it brings with it evils as great as its undue neglect. The body then gradually swallows up the mind; the whole man swells with the pride of conscious strength; by degrees his courage sinks into brutality, and his high spirit into insolence; his senses, the windows of the mind, are clogged and darkened, and his intelligence, neglected and starved, grows 'weak, deaf, and blind'. The problem then of education is to adjust these two complementary but conflicting elements in human nature. The soul is like a stringed instrument, and education has to tune it, tightening here and slackening there, that it may become one instead of many, and its life a harmony instead of a

Each operating on the 'philosophic' element and the element of 'spirit'; and preserving a balance

discord. The man who can thus educate himself or others, who can 'combine music and gymnastic, and apply them in due proportion to the soul', deserves, far more than any musician, to be called a 'musical' man.

Literature as a part of 'music'

Of the two branches of education, 'music', in its widest sense, will clearly begin before 'gymnastic', for we tell stories to children before they can take athletic exercise. The means employed by 'music' in the Platonic system are literature, music proper, and the other fine arts. Each of these, in its different way, is capable of expressing certain ethical characteristics, and by each these characteristics are conveyed, through the eye or ear, to the soul. Of the various means, literature, in the shape of stories and poetry, naturally comes first, and the questions which Plato raises regarding the educational use of literature are two, firstly, what should it express? and secondly, how should it express it? The first question explains itself; the second concerns literary form or style, and, as the ethical influence of form depends mainly, in Plato's view, on the degree to which it is dramatic, this question to him comes to be, How far is the dramatic element in literature good or bad for education? Such a problem would not arise until a comparatively late stage, for in young children the susceptibility to literary influence is as yet too embryonic to admit such distinctions as dramatic or undramatic, personal or impersonal, and the like. The first question then is not as to the form but as to the substance of literature, regarded as an educational agent.

'In all work the beginning is of the greatest impor-

tance, especially when we have to do with a young
and tender creature, for then, more than at any other
time, it receives the particular fashion and stamp
which we wish to impress upon it,' and so, 'what the
child hears when it is young generally becomes fixed
fast and indelibly in its mind.' This is Plato's reason
for giving so much consideration to the beginnings of
education. The young soul, like the young body, is
plastic and malleable, and mothers and nurses, who
take such care that their children's limbs shall grow
straight, should remember how much more care is
needed in the handling and shaping of their minds.
What then are the ideas which should be impressed
most deeply on the minds of children? Speaking
generally, they will be such as we should wish them
to retain when they are grown up. The education of
childhood should lay a foundation of character which
will not have to be cut away as years go on, but
will invite and sustain the superstructure of manhood.
Such a foundation Plato would see laid in certain
religious or semi-religious ideas; he would, in other
words, have the fundamental elements of character
developed in the first instance by habitually putting
before the minds of the young the true nature of God
and of what is most godlike in man. In this sense,
that he would represent the primary moral ideas to
children as embodied in divine or superhuman beings,
Plato may be truly said to invest those ideas with a
religious sanction, and to give his system of education
a religious basis. The child is to be bred up in the
belief that beings greater and better than himself have

What are the ideas that Litera- ture should impress on young minds?

True ideas about God and the godlike in man

behaved in a certain way, and his natural impulse to imitate is thus to be utilized in forming his own character. It would, however, be an inversion of the real order of Plato's thought, to say that he conceives the ideas in question to owe their validity to their superhuman embodiment. On the contrary, it is clear that with him the moral is the criterion of the supernatural, not the supernatural of the moral; and that if, and so far as, a religious sanction means a sanction derived from a story of miraculous events, he considers that sanction to belong to a rudimentary stage of education and intelligence. This will appear more plainly if we examine the form in which what we may call religious truth is supposed by him to be imparted. Education, Plato says, must begin with literature, and 'literature is of two kinds, true and false; it is with the latter kind that education must begin, for the literature which we read to children consists of myths, and myths, speaking generally, are false, though they contain elements of truth as well'. The whole circle of Greek religious ideas, so far as they found expression in language at all, did so mainly in the form of myths. Instead of an authorized collection of more or less historical books, with a mass of authorized doctrine more or less directly depending upon it, the Greeks had a number of floating mythical stories, local and national, some of which, receiving glorified shape from the genius of poets or artists, exercised a special ascendancy over the popular imagination. The bulk of these stories Plato unhesitatingly pronounces 'false', and what he means by 'false' appears from a passage where he is enumerating the cases in which 'falsehood in speech' may be useful and admissible. One of these cases is the 'falsehood of the poet'; for 'in mythology, owing to our ignorance of the actual truth of what happened long ago, we make the falsehood as like the truth as we possibly can, and so render it useful'. The old myths, then, are untrue, not because they necessarily misrepresent facts, but because the lapse of time prevents us from knowing whether any facts underlie them, and what those facts are. They are like pictures of which we are no longer able to test the accuracy. And yet, in the same sentence which tells us that myths are false because we do not know the truth of what they say, we are told that we can 'make them like the truth'. The explanation of this apparent contradiction is found in an important distinction in the sense of falsehood. In the sense that they can at best be only an uncertain approximation to the truth, all myths and mythic poetry are necessarily untrue. They may, however, be untrue in another, and, to Plato, more serious sense; they may not only veil our want of historical knowledge, they may also contradict our fundamental ideas about the subjects of which they treat; they may be not only unhistorical, but morally or metaphysically inconsistent and illogical. Their subject-matter is the divine nature, gods and demigods; of this nature we must have a more or less definite conception, and wherever a myth contradicts that conception, we must pronounce it false. It is in this sense that Plato speaks of the poet 'telling his falsehood badly', 'when he makes

Stories embodying false ideas of this must be excluded

a bad likeness in language of the characters of gods and heroes, like a painter who paints a picture not at all like what he means to copy'. And he gives numerous illustrations of his meaning; the dismal accounts of Hades are 'not true'; the stories of the changes of Proteus and Thetis, of the robberies of Theseus and Peirithous, are 'calumnies'; and it is a sort of 'blasphemy' against Achilles to say or to believe that he was so avaricious as to accept Agamemnon's presents, and not to give up the body of Hector without a price. In one sense, then (to recapitulate), all myths must be false, in so far as we cannot know whether they represent what actually happened; in another sense they may be true or false, according as they do or do not conform to the logical laws of their subject-matter. And as Plato seems to consider myths to be the appropriate form for speaking of the divine nature, when it has to be spoken of as a person or persons, he would seem to conceive of specifically religious truth, so far as it implies such a personal representation, as belonging to a rudimentary stage of mental development. On the other hand, he clearly sees no objection to employing this admittedly inadequate form of expression as an agent in education, nor to telling children religious stories which cannot pretend to be historical.

Moral truth the primary consideration

This entire subordination of historical to moral truth in religious education, strange as it may seem to us, was natural to Plato. The mythology which occupied the Greek mind was its own creation, the offspring of its early contact with nature, developed by subsequent reflection; and the mind from which it sprang felt itself competent to judge it. The element of dogmatic fixity in their religion attached much more to its ritual than to its ideas; these latter were a plastic material, growing in accordance with the secret laws of psychology and language, or the conscious design of poets. In applying to them canons of criticism resting on no authority but that of his own moral consciousness, Plato might expect to offend many popular beliefs and prejudices, but they would not be the beliefs or prejudices of a priesthood or a church. It seems to be incident to religious movements and ideas, that they rapidly gather round them an accretion of mythical events and conceptions, and neither the Jewish nor the Christian religion is an exception to the general rule. But there is this great difference between them and the Greek religion, that the literature to which the former attach themselves, large as is its infusion of poetry and mythology, still purports in its most important parts to be historical and that with its historical character its religious significance has come to be almost inseparably associated. And thus, in religious education, we are not only met by the question which Plato asked, Whether the whole of this literature is consistent with our ideas of the divine nature? but we have also to settle the question, which did not present itself to Plato, Whether it is consistent with our canons of historical evidence? Had Plato been writing now, he would have found the second a more prominent question than the first, and we cannot say with certainty what his advice would have been to

Criticism of Greek mythology involved in this

those who find themselves in the dilemma of teaching, or seeing others teach, their children religious stories which they themselves do not believe to be true. We may, however, conjecture that he would have made the moral worth of those stories the final test, and that if they had seemed to him to embody ideas really vital to human life and character, he would have retained them, trusting to the child's mind to assimilate what was valuable, and to later education to preserve or to rectify its sense of historical truth.

The increased appreciation of the distinction between truth of fact and truth of idea, is often and rightly represented as a characteristic of modern, as compared with ancient, thought. Yet, in its ultimate analysis, the distinction is seen to exist only in abstraction. Neither 'mere' facts nor 'mere' ideas form any part of our knowledge, but facts which are interpreted into our mental experience, and ideas which are referred to something independent of that experience. The importance of an historical fact must depend, in the last resort, upon its moral or ideal significance, or, in other words, upon what it tells us of our own nature; and our conception of the use and value of evidence is in advance of that of the Greeks, not because we have discovered a new sort of truth which was unknown to them, but because our whole mental horizon has enormously expanded, and we are far more vividly conscious of the possible bearings of one part of our experience upon another. Our truth of fact is more pregnant with thought than theirs, and our truth of idea goes back into a deeper reality.

We have seen in what sense Plato bases education What is the truth about God which Literature must teach? on religion, and how he conceives that the mythical form in which religious ideas are presented may be, in different ways, both true and untrue. The next question is, What is that religious truth which mythical literature may approximately express, and by its conformity to which its educational value is to be determined? Clearly it can be no other than the most perfect and consistent conception which can be formed of the divine nature. Plato accordingly begins by laying down certain 'outlines of theology, which the makers of stories must not be allowed to transgress', for 'God must always be represented as he really is, whether in epic or in tragedy'. The doctrines of Plato's state-religion are only two, but they go to the root of the matter; the first is, that God is good and the cause of good only; the second is, that God is unchangeable and true. Thus simply stated, they are the common property of all higher religious thought, but Plato's application of them is to some extent peculiar. The primitive conception of the deity as The two leading doctrines the simple embodiment of power, readily leads in one direction to the belief that he sends good and evil upon man according to his caprice, and in another to the idea that he is jealous of human success. To these deep-rooted tenets of the Greek popular religion Plato opposes the simple logical position, that what is in its essence good cannot produce what is not good. As to the difficulty of accounting for the undoubted preponderance of evil in the world, 'either we must say that it is not the work of God; or that, if the work

of God, its infliction is just and good, and those who
suffer it are the better for being chastised. . . . To say
that bad men are miserable because they need
chastisement is allowable, but not to say that God is
the cause of their misery.' In the emphasis with which
Plato insists on this truth, we see not only the resolu-
tion of the philosopher to uphold his logical conception
of the divine nature, but also the anxiety of the legislator and teacher to press home human responsibility.
To encourage the natural tendency to lay to the door
of an irresponsible being the evil which we ourselves
have caused or deserved, is what no state will do 'if
it is to be well governed'. In the oracular words of
the daughter of Necessity to the souls about to enter
on their earthly life, 'Virtue owns no master; as a man
honours or dishonours her he will have more or less
of her. The guilt is with him who chooses. God is
guiltless.'

The application of the other great religious principle is still more strongly coloured by Greek or
Platonic ideas. The liability to change by external
influences, whether in organic bodies, or in products
of art, or in the human soul itself, seems to Plato a
universal symptom of inferiority or weakness; least
of all in the divine being, the absolutely best, can he
admit any variableness. Nor again in another and
more obvious sense can he conceive of God as liable
to change. The metamorphoses which play so large
a part in the stories about the Greek divinities are
impossible to a being who is already perfect; for no
one, God or man, will voluntarily change for the

worse. It is not the representation of the deity as having shape or similitude which offends Plato, as it did the great Jewish teachers, but the indignity offered to the divine essence by supposing it capable of wantonly taking lower forms. Lastly, it is inconceivable that God should be otherwise than true, whether in the peculiarly Platonic sense of untruth, in which it means want of conformity in the mind to fact, ignorance of that which it is vital to know, the 'delusion' which makes us 'believe a lie', or in the ordinary sense of deceiving others by word or deed. In the first sense no man, much less God, could choose to be untrue; in the latter, there are some circumstances under which men think lying admissible, but none of these circumstances can apply to God.

Such is Plato's conception of the divine nature; and as such, in its essence and its operation, he would have it presented by poets to the imagination of his future citizens, 'if they are to be men who reverence God and are like God as far as it is possible for man to be so'. These general religious ideas, however, are not the only ideas which he would see embodied in poetry, and by which he would judge of its right to a place in the education of a people. It should be its function also to exhibit the moral ideal in all its various manifestations; and we have next to ask how Plato conceived of that ideal, and what are the specific qualities and principles which he considered to be at once the true elements of moral greatness, and the legitimate material of poetical art. Plato's 'whole duty of man' is comprised in the following list: honour to

The general duty of poetry to show forth the moral ideal

Qualities
of which
Plato
thought
this ideal
is com-
posed parents, love of fellow citizens, courage, truthfulness, self-control. Each of these deserves a few words of notice. The honour due to father and mother is set by Plato next to the honour due to the gods, and he denounces the stories of the treatment of Cronos by his son Zeus as 'the greatest of lies about the greatest things'. The mixed sentiment of awe, admiration, and modesty, which the Greeks associated with the untranslatable word αἰδώς, and which they regarded as the germ of all youthful virtue, has its earliest and simplest expression in the feeling of children for their parents; and to diffuse this feeling through society, knitting old and young together by an instinctive bond, and superseding the law of the state by the finer law of family affection, was one of the fairest though most impossible dreams of Plato's life. Equally important in his eyes was the sense of fellowship amongst citizens. The false tales of the battles of the gods with one another are not to be told to children, who should see in the Olympian community the glorified image of their own. Rather they are to be taught that it is 'very disgraceful lightly to quarrel amongst themselves', 'that citizen never falls out with citizen, and that it is wicked to do it'. Thus the earliest lessons of education are to appeal to that element in the soul which, as we have seen, Plato regarded as the highest and most distinctively human in man, the element in virtue of which he is not a mere isolated atom and centre of resistance, but capable of attraction both to what is higher than himself and to what is like himself.

From the common groundwork of citizenlike feeling
we pass to the specific virtues of public life, and
the first of these is courage, or, as we might more
literally and more instructively translate the Greek
word ἀνδρεία, 'manliness'. Plato's treatment of this
quality is characteristically Greek. The child who
is to be one day a soldier and to fight for his country
must learn before all things not to be afraid of death.
Death, as the inevitable end of youth and strength
and beauty, as the entrance to a joyless and ineffectual
phantom world, seemed to the Greek imagination of
all terrible things the most terrible, and the man who
could face it without flinching the most worthy to be
called a man. Plato, as usual, has both a speculative
and a practical interest in banishing from poetry the
ghastly pictures of Hades; they 'are not true', and they
'do no good'. 'Not true', for to Plato it is clear that a
good man can have no reason for being afraid of death;
and 'they do no good', for whatever scope they may
give to descriptive power, and however pleasant it
may be to feel the pulse quicken and the skin creep
at reading them, they only unnerve the character,
and are bad for children who are to learn 'to be free-
men, fearing slavery worse than death'. But if a man
need not be afraid to die himself, neither need he be
afraid for his friend to die, and the expenditure of
tears and lamentations over the departed is both
uncalled for and unmanly, for a man ought to learn
as far as possible to lean upon himself, not upon others.
And if it is weak to give way to excess of grief, it is no
less so to give way to the opposite emotion; laughter,

like tears, is not to be allowed to get the better of us, for the violent expression of one feeling tends to produce an equally violent reaction.

These precepts, to which Plato is led by his conception of moral truth, remind us of those which Lessing arrived at by thinking out the laws of artistic propriety. Perhaps few Englishmen will feel themselves or their children to be much in need of such precepts. Many of us would be only too glad sometimes if our sense of the pathetic or the ludicrous could find more relief in expression. To the Greek of Plato's time, as to some southern peoples now, the tendency to sudden and violent revulsions of feeling was a real cause and symptom of weakness of character. (To us, taught as we are from early years by example and temperament to be neutral and moderate in our language and gesture, an analogous danger may perhaps be found in the tendency to nurse suppressed emotion until it becomes a drain upon the mental forces or breaks out in extravagant action.

In his treatment of truthfulness, the virtue which comes next upon his list, Plato is short and simple. Elsewhere, in passages where truth is identified with 'what is', we find him basing the obligation to truthfulness upon the desire to be in harmony with fact; here, where he is concerned primarily with early education, he connects it naturally with obedience. He would have the young citizens continually conscious that they are living under authority, and that 'to say the thing that is not' to their elders is as 'deadly and destructive to the community' as it would be for the sailor to lie to his officer or the patient to his doctor. Obedience too is the basis of the remaining virtue of σωφροσύνη, which in its literal sense describes the man who remains 'sound in mind', or, as we might say, 'keeps his head', under the stress of appetite and passion. 'To obey those who are in authority and to have authority over one's self' is the fully developed virtue of which the sentiment of αἰδώς is the instinctive germ. It is this law-loving spirit, whether the law be the external law of the state or the voice of reason within us, which is the enemy alike of forwardness and insolence, of gluttony, drunkenness, and lust, of meanness and avarice. The principle of balance and control, which so pervades the Greek life and philosophy, comes out nowhere so prominently as in the conception of this virtue. It is a principle which no longer appeals strongly to the modern mind, to which it tends to suggest rather the complacencies and prettinesses of morality than its inward victories or struggles. But to a people like the Greeks, combining such an extraordinary sense of proportion with such an extraordinary capacity for excess, a perfect self-mastery might well seem as high an ideal as the humility and purity which take its place in the Christian code.

The elements of moral greatness just enumerated form the second main category in the legitimate material of poetry in a well-ordered state. To trace them out in the lives and actions of national heroes and great men, and to give them fitting expression, is the true function of the masters of language. The

In dealing with human life also, poets must keep to the truth divine and the heroic, however, are not the only subjects which Plato would allow to poets. There remains the whole sphere of human life and nature, to discover some principle in which was the original problem of the *Republic*. How then are poets to deal with this vast material? What canons can be laid down to which their imagination should conform in drawing human nature, corresponding to the canons of religious and moral truth which they are not to transgress in drawing the divine? Is the world really what it is popularly represented, a scene of confusion and caprice, in which the unjust are happy and the just miserable? The answer to these questions is the *Republic* itself. If, as Plato would have us believe, justice is the health, and injustice the disease, of human life, individual and social; if the triumph of what is most divine in the world is also the triumph of what is most human, and man can only realize himself by living at his highest; if the life of the just man is in the hand of God, who orders all things for good whatever the appearances may be, and if, when we come to look at the facts, even in the judgement of the world justice more often prospers than not; if this is the truth, then children must be taught it, and poets must sing it, and the contrary representations of popular literature are as great calumnies upon man as they are upon gods and heroes.

Many reflections must be suggested to a modern reader of the part of the *Republic* to which we have been referring, partly as regards the nature and the method of early education, and partly also as regards

What is the truth?

Supreme importance attached to the

the position and functions of poetry and literature. One of the first points which must strike him, accustomed as he is to hear the methods of imparting knowledge, and the kind of knowledge to be imparted, made the main subjects of discussion, is the almost exclusive attention given by Plato to the method of developing character, and the kind of character to be developed. We are not indeed to suppose that Plato intended children to be brought up in ignorance of reading, writing, and arithmetic; besides this elementary knowledge, he evidently contemplated some teaching of the rudiments of such science as then existed. But he does not dwell upon this early scientific education, except to say that it will be comparatively unsystematic, and that it should be made as little compulsory as possible, 'for the acquisition of knowledge ought not to be made a slavery to any free man'. Thus it remains true on the whole that Plato regarded the formation of character in childhood and early youth as a much more important part of education than useful instruction or the training of the intellect. It would, however, be a mistake to suppose that because this branch of education finds a comparatively small place in modern theoretical discussions, it is therefore neglected in modern practice; on the contrary, it is probably just because it receives so much attention at home and at school, that it is thought capable of taking care of itself. The successes of our public-school system have lain, much more than in any particular stimulus that they have given to literary or scientific activity, in the production

development of a certain type of character

Greek and English practice compared

of certain types of character and the preparation for the art of life, and in these points we naturally feel less need for method or even for consistency. And yet perhaps our very feeling of security should make us diffident. The names of 'Christian', 'scholar', and 'gentleman', are as much in our mouths as those of the cardinal virtues were in the mouths of the Greeks; but the ideas of religion, culture, and manhood, which we attach to them, are not less confused, and often not less untrue, than some of those which Plato found in the current literature and opinion of his day.

Our neglect of the theory of ethical education as compared with Plato has also another explanation. In a small Greek State, with the whole or greater part of its effective citizens taking part in the conduct of affairs, the influence of personal character upon society and politics was more direct and unmistakable than it can be in the vast organization of a modern nation, where the members at the circumference may be almost unconscious of their connexion with the centre. Ultimately, no doubt, it is as true now as it was in the times of Plato and Aristotle that the character of a people is responsible for its social and political life, and that education is mainly important because it produces or modifies that character and thus affects the public interests. But the steps by which ethical and psychological agencies come to the surface in politics are much more numerous now and much more difficult to trace, and it is proportionately more easy to isolate particular aspects of the national life and to treat them as if they had no connexion with each other or the whole. And thus, while it has become a commonplace that many of the evils of modern society can only be cured by education, few people probably can see the connexion between the evil and the remedy as clearly, and express it as simply, as Plato did when he said that the encouragement of ghostly fears and superstitions tends to make bad soldiers, or that changes of fashion in popular music are symptoms of political revolution.

But the difference between ourselves and Plato in the relative importance attached to the education of character is not greater than the difference in the means employed for that education. In the first place, we have no really national mythology which takes, or could be made to take, such a position in education as did that of the Greek people. The Arthur legend has indeed been recently made to yield the picture of an 'ideal knight', and the still more recent treatment of the Scandinavian Sagas has shown that the ideas which stirred our forefathers are still alive in ourselves. But the position of Mr. Tennyson and Mr. Morris in this respect is very different from that of the Greek dramatists. The myths with which the latter worked had been handed down by a continuous tradition, both literary and popular; and however freely a poet might transform or modernize them, he was still sure of appealing to the popular imagination, of which his material had come to form an integral part. The characters of Celtic and Scandinavian mythology are no longer domesticated amongst us; we no longer regard them with either familiarity or

How can the type be produced?

Influence of mythology in ancient and modern times

reverence; the ties which bound them to us have been shattered beyond repair, and it is only here and there that we dimly catch sight of them behind the crowd of classical and Christian figures which has pressed in between us and them.

The Bible   The place thus left vacant in education by our want of a national mythology has been partially filled by other forms of literature, of which the books of the Old and New Testaments are the most conspicuous, while alongside of them there has grown up the miscellaneous mass of stories, romances, allegories, and fairy-tales, comprised under the head of 'literature for the young'. It is from these two sources that our early conceptions of the divine and the heroic are mainly derived. What would Plato have thought of them? He would no doubt have been surprised at the hard-and-fast line which it is usual to draw between sacred and profane literature, which robs the former of much of its legitimate literary effect, and the latter of much of its educational power. There may seem to be a certain incongruity in applying high canons of criticism to the story-books of children; and indeed their miscellaneous character and rapid multiplication makes such an application almost impossible. Yet it would be a fruitful work for a competent person to make such a collection from the religious books, mythologies, and popular tales of different peoples and ages, as should appeal to and stimulate the best elements in a child's imagination, without either spoiling its simplicity, over-exciting its sensibility, or nursing its conceit. In such a collection the most appropriate stories from the Bible would find their natural place. The circumstances which have led to the biblical writings being treated as a single book, while investing them all with the same promiscuous sanctity, have greatly increased the difficulty of using them as a text-book of religion and morality. There is much in the Old Testament which Plato's canons would exclude from the education of the young, and some of the worst expressions of Jewish fanaticism have served as the watchwords of modern cruelty or cant. On the other hand, the direct influence of example is much less in the case of the Old Testament than it was in that of the Greek poets. The heroes of Jewish history do not live in the English mind as types to be imitated in the same way that the Greek heroes lived in the mind of their own nation. It is to the words with which their names are associated, rather than to the deeds, that the influence of the former is due, and this makes it all the more important that their words should be purged from the baser matter which adheres to them, and fitted to be in truth what they are now only in name, a revelation of the divine nature to the English people. With the New Testament the case is different. Here it is the story of a life and a character to which, more than to anything else, the power of the book has been due; and Plato, if he might have warned us gently against that literal imitation which is really no imitation, would have found there all and more than all the ideal of heroic manhood which he sought for in vain in the figures of his native mythology. And yet

we must see that the very exaltation of that character
and life makes it difficult to present it to children
without falsifying it, and that we are not teaching
them to be like Jesus, either on the one hand by
making him so familiar to them that they can 'play
at being him', or on the other by introducing him
to them in a buckram of ecclesiastical dogma. To us,
as to Plato, the problem of early religious education
is, How to express the highest truth in the most
appropriate and the least inadequate forms. But in
the interval of more than two thousand years which
separates us from him, the spiritual inheritance of
Europe has been both enormously enriched and
enormously encumbered; enriched by the advent and
expansion of new and potent religious ideas, which
have carried the human mind to heights scarcely
dreamt of by him, but encumbered also by an under-
growth of theological tangle which makes it harder
for us to keep in view the grander outlines of the truth
and the light towards which they tend.

The task
assigned
to the
poets

The demand of Plato that poets should be teachers,
and their subject-matter limited accordingly, will
generally be received with disgust or derision in the
republic of letters. This is due partly to the extreme
simplicity and even crudity of Plato's language, and
the difficulty of translating it to suit the complex
conditions of our modern civilization, partly to a
narrow conception of the scope of education on the
one hand and the responsibilities of literature on the
other. Plato in the *Republic*, as he tells us himself, 'is
not making poetry, but founding a commonwealth,

and the founder should know the outlines within
which the invention of poets should be exercised; but
it is not his business to invent himself'. Hence to any
one who thinks of the exuberant variety of the poetic
activity, these 'outlines' are apt to seem a Procrustes-
bed, and Plato's poet is pictured as a literary tailor
who cuts his wares to order. And this feeling is in-
tensified by the fact that Plato is much more concerned
to criticise the current literature of his time than to
suggest fresh lines for writers to work on, thus leaving
the impression of an entirely hostile attitude to poetry
in general. Moreover, in reading proposals like his,
we are naturally more apt to seize upon the difficulties
or mistakes in them than on the essential truth which
they may contain. We are all agreed that a public
censorship of poetry would be impossible and self-
destructive; we also see that as a matter of fact the
greatest poets have not often been educators of their
people. We forget that this idea of a censorship is an
accident of Plato's mind and circumstances, and
that the truest ideas are often those which are most
slowly realized in history. For what is the requirement here made, if we look at it on its positive, not
merely its negative, side? It is that the poet should
take his place in the commonwealth, not as an orna-
mental luxury, a caterer for the pleasure of intellectual
epicures, but as an integral part of it, with a work of
his own, imprinting the first indelible ideas upon the
souls of the young, revealing the inscrutable nature
of God in forms of imaginative truth, nerving the
heart and chastening the emotions by the power of

heroic examples, interpreting to the fancy the language of facts, and surrounding the mind with an atmosphere of health and beauty. This is not a position of which any poet need be ashamed. Few, if any, have ever risen to it; but not a few, and those not the least, have claimed it. 'The abilities of the poet,' says Milton, 'wheresoever they be found, are the inspired gift of God, rarely bestowed, but yet to some —though most abuse—in every nation: and are of power, besides the office of a pulpit, to inbreed and cherish in a great people the seeds of virtue and public civility; to allay the perturbations of the mind, and set the affections in right tune; to celebrate in glorious and lofty hymns the throne and equipage of God's almightiness, and what he suffers to be wrought with high providence in his church; to sing victorious agonies of martyrs and saints, the deeds and triumphs of just and pious nations, doing valiantly through faith against the enemies of Christ; to deplore the general relapses of kingdoms and states from justice and God's true worship. Lastly, whatsoever in religion is holy and sublime, in virtue amiable or grave, whatsoever hath passion or admiration in all the changes of that which is called fortune from without, or the wily subtleties and refluxes of man's thoughts from within; all these things, with a solid and treatable smoothness, to point out and describe.'

High words like these will perhaps provoke a smile or a sigh in those who remember the bathos of unsuccessful attempts to carry them into effect; and when to this is added the thought of the pressure of modern life, so feverish and yet so mechanical, so interesting and yet so unlovely, the poet himself will sometimes lose heart, and become, instead of 'the trumpet which sings to battle', 'the idle singer of an empty day'. Yet those who fancy that the lamp of imagination is waning before the dawn of industry and science might reflect that our scientific insight into nature is scarcely more in advance of the crude fancies of the Greeks than our imaginative interpretation of it is in advance of their naïve mythology. And if others are inclined to retire to a 'shadowy isle of bliss', and to leave education to school boards and ministers, they should remember that the 'immortal garland' of poetry must be 'run for, not without dust and heat'. They might consider, too (to adapt Milton's words once more), 'What nation it is whereof they are, and whereof' (if they knew it) 'they are the governors; a nation not slow and dull, but of a quick, ingenious, and piercing spirit; acute to invent, subtile and sinewy to discourse, not beneath the reach of any point that human capacity can soar to'. Such a nation is worthy to be educated by men who have the genius to do it.

We have heard Plato's answer to the first of the two questions which he raised about poets—the question, What ought they to say? and may now pass on to the second, How ought they to say it? What is the manner or form of poetry best fitted to the functions which have been assigned to it in education? By the form of poetry Plato understands merely the mode in which the poet represents the personages in his poem, that is, whether

What is the form of poetry best suited to our purpose?

he speaks in his own person and simply describes what
they say and do, or whether he puts himself in their
place and makes them speak and act for themselves.
The first of these manners he calls 'narrative', the
second 'imitative'; the two may of course be employed
separately, or combined in various proportions in the
same work. The type of the 'imitative' manner is the
drama, that of the 'narrative' certain kinds of choric
hymns, while the epic introduces them both. We
shall, however, understand Plato better if we banish
from our minds this triple division of poetry, with its
modern associations, and fix them upon the real
question which occupied him. That question is,
Whether 'imitation', or, as we might better say, im-
personation, should be the ruling principle in poetry,
or whether some other principle should rule; or, in
other words, Is the poet to put himself into as
many and as various interesting personalities and
situations as he possibly can, and is the greatest poet
he who can do this to the greatest extent, or is he
to observe some principle of selection other than
that of the merely interesting, and is there some other
criterion of poetic excellence than the degree of
'imitative' power? That this is the real issue in Plato's
mind appears from the following passage: 'The well-
regulated man, when he comes in his narrative to a
speech or a deed of a good man, will, it seems to me,
want to give it in the very person of that man, and of
such imitation he will not be ashamed; he will imitate the good man most of all, when he acts without
stumbling or folly; to a less extent and degree when

he has been upset by disease, or love, or drunkenness, or any other calamity. But when he comes
upon a person unworthy of himself, he will not like
seriously to assimilate himself to his inferior, unless it
be on the few occasions when he does something good;
partly he is unpractised in imitating such people, and
partly, too, it goes against the grain to put himself into
the mould of natures worse than his own; his mind
scorns to do such a thing, unless it be in fun.' On the
other hand, 'the lower the nature of the poet, the less
will he discriminate in what he says, or think anything
unworthy of him, so that he will try to imitate anything and everything, in sober earnest and before a
large audience, such things even as thunder and wind
and hail, the noises of wheels and pulleys, the tones
of trumpets, flutes, pipes, and all kinds of instruments,
and the voices of dogs, sheep, and birds'. We see that
Plato is here grouping together forms of imitation
which would be distinguished by a modern writer.
As art and literature advance, the primitive delight
of mere mimicry gives way to that of subtler kinds of
reproduction, and tends to confine itself to the less
educated classes of society. But though the dramatic
poet stands on a different level from the actor, still
more from the pantomimist, they all agree in one
point, that they are endowed with more than ordinary
capacity of losing their own personality in that of
others. It is in this common capacity that Plato sees a
danger, a danger both to the artist who possesses it, and,
in various degrees, to the audience which is able to
follow him in the exercise of it. His whole conception

Varieties of 'imitation'

of the true form of human society is based, as we saw, on the principle that each member in it should have his work to do, and should do it. He is convinced of the impossibility of one man's excelling in many trades or professions; the same natural law which makes every man the possible helpmate of others imposes on him the necessity of accepting help from them. And if one man cannot do many things well, neither can he imitate many things; and Plato (at least when he wrote the *Republic*) did not think it possible for the same poet, or even for the same actor, to excel both in tragedy and comedy. This law of the limitation of human nature, which he found to hold good in arts and professions, he would see observed in the greatest of all arts and professions, the life of the citizen who is engaged in the public service of the state. To men for whom the good of the commonwealth is to be the paramount rule of conduct, whose 'craft' is to be to maintain the liberty of their country, what need is there of doing or being anything except what bears upon their work? and if not of doing and being, why of imitating? For imitation, bodily or mental, cannot remain mere imitation; if it begin early and continue long, it results in a second nature. If, then, the young are to put themselves into other characters at all, let it be such characters as we wish them ultimately to be, but no others, 'lest from the imitation they catch something of the reality'. And thus the only poets who will have work to do in a well-ordered State, will be those who will 'imitate what is right, and that only'; who will express in their works the true type of character, and thereby help to produce it. As for the great pantomimic genius, 'the man with the skill to turn himself into all kinds of people, and to imitate everything', he may be allowed to be 'divine and miraculous and delightful'; but he will find no audience in a society where 'twofold and manifold men do not exist, but everybody does one thing'.

The mitigated attack made upon the drama in the third book of the *Republic*, is renewed by Plato in the tenth with greater vehemence and a more elaborate array of argument. We need not here enter into the general theory of the nature of artistic production which he there advances in order to refute the extravagant claims of omniscience made for the poets by their admirers; but his account of the psychological effects of dramatic poetry may be noticed, as it develops and illustrates that given in the earlier book. Plato charges dramatic writers, firstly, with depending mainly upon illusion for their success; and secondly, with weakening character by over-stimulating the emotions. The meaning of the first charge is best seen from the analogy of painting by which it is illustrated. Painting and kindred arts produce their effects by taking advantage of certain optical illusions; the perception of the actual proportions of objects is kept in abeyance by the mere appearance, until corrected by scientific measurement. Similarly the poet takes advantage of illusions of feeling; the aspects of character which he likes to represent are not those where it is simple, quiet, consistent, and rational, but rather its emotional aspects, with their shifting lights and

Danger to the development of character arising out of dramatic poetry

shadows, where the contrasts are strong and the
transitions rapid; and the element in his audience to
which he appeals, and upon which he reckons for his
success, is not the sober judgement which sees life in
its true proportions, but the illusory feelings of the
moment which care only for their immediate satisfaction. So that, judged by the worth both of what it
represents and of what it appeals to, dramatic poetry
seems to condemn itself to inferiority. The second
charge against it is an expansion of that made in the
third book. Few people reflect that in putting themselves in the positions of others, they catch something
which becomes their own. Yet this is the case when,
in seeing tragedy and comedy, we give unrestrained
way to emotions which we should be ashamed to
indulge in real life. We think it does not matter,
because we stand outside the circumstances which call
them forth; but when similar circumstances arise in
our own experience we find that our will has been
weakened and our self-respect undermined.

The two
prime
duties,
both over-
looked by
the drama Two dominant ideas underlie all the objections
urged by Plato against the dramatic element in litera-
ture: the duty of being true to ourselves, and the duty
of being true to facts. The two were in his mind closely
related. As the burden of his philosophy of knowledge
was that we should learn to see things as they are, not
as they appear to us to be, so the burden of his philosophy of conduct is that we should learn to be what
we really are, and not what our fancy makes us. And
as the belief in an objective world of reality, an order
of existence which we do not create, but which we

find and must recognize, pervades his logical speculation, so it is the corresponding conviction that the
rational self in man is his most real self, and that life
in accordance with the rational order of the world is
his truest life, which gives nerve and consistency to
his theories of morality. We have already seen expressions of this conviction in the denial of the possibility of change in the divine nature, and in the
condemnation of excessive indulgence of emotion.
Order and immutability seemed to Plato the attributes of what is best and highest both in the physical
and in the moral world, and it is just these attributes
which he missed in the capricious current of feeling.
The lower he went in human nature or in human
society, the more did he seem to find men the creatures
of their sentiment, and the less purpose or law did he
discern in their lives. And art, especially dramatic
art, seemed to him to pander to this natural fickleness.
It had no principle of selection, no law of better and
worse; wherever it could raise a laugh, or draw a sigh,
or tickle an appetite, there it was ready with its phan-
tasmagoria of life. It had a direct interest in 'watering
and nourishing' the lower and more trivial impulses
which reason calls upon us 'to dry up', and it stimulated the already too great tendency in us to do everybody's business except our own, to be actors instead
of citizens, to play at life instead of living it. The words
of Bacon, in which he gives the reason why poetry
'was ever thought to have some participation of
divineness', might have been used by Plato in another
sense to express why it is so far from being divine;

'poetry doth raise and erect the mind, by submitting the shows of things to the desires of the mind, whereas reason doth buckle and bow the mind unto the nature of things.'

Relevance
of this
criticism
for our
own time The very emphasis and fullness of Plato's polemic against dramatic literature must make us feel that he was writing in a different atmosphere from our own. Few modern writers on education in England would reckon the stage amongst the most powerful agents, whether for good or bad; few too would regard a tendency to theatricality and effusiveness as one of the most serious dangers to the English character. Not the most extravagant admirer of our dramatists would claim for them what Plato heard men claim for Homer, that they have 'educated their country, and deserve to be read over and over again as authorities on human conduct and education, and as models on which men may order the whole of their lives'. Nor is the average Englishman likely to be too 'imitative' in the sense which alarmed Plato. The suppleness of nature which made it hard for the Athenian to be 'one man and not many', is generally replaced in us by a sturdiness and concentration, of which consistency and self-respect, self-consciousness and selfishness, are respectively the good and the bad developments. Yet it must be admitted that these qualities are not incompatible with illusions and extravagances of feeling, none the less dangerous because outwardly repressed; and though we are not, on the whole, a nation of theatregoers, we are undoubtedly a nation of novel-readers, and may find there the dramatic stimulants against

which Plato protested. It must be borne in mind, in comparing any ethical influence of literature in ancient and modern times, that what in Greece was mainly a public of spectators and listeners is now mainly a public of readers. It is true that in the pulpit we have a medium of oral communication which they had not, but, speaking generally, it is not now in the open places of the theatre, the camp, the law-courts, and the market-place, that the uttered word most circulates and works; it is rather in silence or in solitude, through the newspaper on the family table, the periodical at the club, the poem or novel in the bed-room, that the modern writer speaks to his fellow men. And the difference in the medium goes along with a difference in the effect. Instead of the noisy publicity in which contagious feeling grows as it spreads from man to man, till the individual is 'borne helplessly along the stream', and loses himself in an indiscriminate froth of exaggerated feeling, we brood over books in the heated cells of our own imagination, build castles of the fumes of our own emotions, and come forth to measure the world by the mock-heroic standard of our own littleness. But the craving for change and excitement, the desire to escape from our own true selves with the responsibilities which they entail, are not the less strong in us because we are not born actors or mimics; the mind can make its own stage and act upon it, while the body remains immobile and unexpressive. Nor does the modern demand exceed the modern supply. The novel, which absorbs so much of our dramatic talent, lends itself with fatal ease to the promiscuous photography of situations and feelings. The increased sense of the importance of human life and of the inexhaustibleness of its problems supplies a ready argument to those who find anything and everything 'interesting'; and there are still writers of whom we might say metaphorically what Plato intended literally, 'that there is nothing which they will not imitate, thunder and wind, trumpets and whistles, dogs and sheep'.

The importance for our purpose of Music (in the usual sense of the word)

The same principles which guided Plato in his conception of the educational function of literature guided him also in his treatment of the other constituents of 'musical' education, and led him to conclusions still more at variance with modern practice and theory. That poetry and literature, which express definite ideas, should be made to serve the interests of society, is an intelligible if surprising proposal; but that music, painting, and sculpture should be pressed into the same service, will seem to many a vague fancy, impracticable in education, and destructive of art. Let us then see what Plato's idea of the use of the arts in education precisely was. 'Music,' he says, 'involves three elements, words, harmony, rhythm', or, as we may say, to bring his meaning nearer home, without pretending to give it an exact modern equivalent, words, key, and time. As to the words, they must conform to the same canons as the words of other poetry, and the character of the two remaining elements must be determined by that of the words. Those 'harmonies' and 'rhythms' then must be employed in musical composition which will express the

qualities which we wish to develop in the soul. What
these are we already know. They are the qualities
which result from the right nurture of the two higher
psychological elements in human nature, the 'spirited'
and the 'philosophic'. We must therefore have a
music of corresponding character, a music of war and
a music of peace, a 'harmony' of violence and effort,
and a 'harmony' of conciliation and calm, a 'harmony'
to represent the daring of the soldier and the endurance of the martyr, and a 'harmony' to express the
accents of entreaty or persuasion, of submission or
acquiescence. Other kinds than these, and other
instruments than these require, are superfluous
luxuries which must be 'purged away' in a healthy
state, whose object is not to stimulate every feverish
craving of its citizens, but to weave strongly those vital
strains of character which sustain the fabric of society.
The same principle will apply to the 'rhythms' and
measures of music and dance, as to the 'harmonies'
in which they are composed; they must not develop
in lawless independence, but must be such as will
express 'the orderly and brave life'.

There is then, according to Plato, a right and a _{Its power}
wrong in the musical relations of pitch and time, and _{the growth}
this right and wrong is in some sense akin to the right _{character}
and wrong in human nature and conduct. Goodness
and badness of form, he says, follow goodness and
badness of rhythm, and goodness and badness of
rhythm follow goodness and badness of language,
and these again depend upon goodness and badness
of character. Nor is it only in the movements of dance

and song that there is this correspondence; in all sensuous material there is a similar capability of expression; it is present in the forms of painting and sculpture, of weaving and embroidery, of building and manufacture, of animal and vegetable life; 'in all of these there is shapeliness or unshapeliness, and unshapeliness and unrhythmicalness and inharmoniousness are the kindred of badness of language and badness of character, while the opposites are kindred and imitations of the opposite character, the chastened and the good'. The poets then are not the only artists over whom the state should exercise control; attention must be given to the whole body of craftsmen, and Similarly with the other arts they must be prevented from expressing what is vicious and unchastened, mean and unshapely, whether in the figures of living things or in buildings or in any other work of art. The artists who should be encouraged by the state must be 'those who have the genius to track out the nature of what is fair and shapely' and to embody it anew in their works. For the young citizens must not be allowed to grow up amongst images of evil, lest their souls by daily contact gradually and unconsciously assimilate the ugliness of their surroundings. Rather they should be like men living in a beautiful and healthy place; from everything that they see and hear, loveliness, like a breeze, should pass into their souls, and teach them without their knowing it the truth of which it is a manifestation. In such an atmosphere they will not only acquire a natural grace and proportion of bearing and character, but an instinctive sense of what is fair and what

is foul in nature and in art; and this instinctive sense
is a kind of anticipation of a rational understanding
of the nature of good and evil; for the reason which is
now presented to them in forms of sense, and calls
forth sensuous delight, is the same reason which they
will afterwards learn to know in its own form as an
intelligible principle, and which they will then recognize as an old friend with a new face.

Such is the nature and such are the limits of the
education of 'music'. It has a more intellectual and
a more emotional aspect. From the former point of
view, it is completed when we have 'learned to read'
the world of sights and sounds which is about us. That
world is like a language which we have got to master;
the sensible forms of good and evil pass and repass
before us in an infinite variety of combinations, like
the letters of an alphabet which combine into an
infinity of words, great and small. No form can be
disregarded; acts and speeches which seem trivial,
like the little words in a book, may contain a world
of meaning and be the key to a character. And the
true function of the artist is to help us to learn this
language of life; he is the man who knows the shapes
of the letters and the laws of their combinations. In
the 'mirror' which he holds up we may see reflected
the images of courage, temperance, generosity, and
their opposites, and thus learn to know the realities
when we see them. Thus art should find its fulfilment
in life; and he may most truly be said to be 'musically'
educated, whose eye and ear are trained to detect
what is right and wrong, not only in the creations of

The influ-
ence of the
arts in the
training of
the intel-
lect

art, but also, so far as it can be apprehended by the
senses, in the actual world of which art is the reflection.

and of the emotions   If, on the other hand, we regard the emotional
effects of 'musical' education, they may be summed
up in two, that it infuses a spirit of order, and that it
develops the 'true love' of beauty, the former being
the more passive condition of which the latter is the
more active expression. To Plato, most of the evils
of sensual passion fall under one of two heads, unregulated variety or unregulated intensity. He considered
passion to be essentially 'many-headed', and capable
of indefinite multiplication and expansion; and one
of his chief charges against the art of his time was that
it fostered and satisfied the indiscriminate craving for
emotional excitement. In contrast with it, he demanded an art which should not merely stimulate,
but should also discipline, the feelings; which should
not follow but lead them; which should chasten their
disorder and brace their indolence by making them
move in the delicate lines of proportion and beauty,
and respond to the quiet emphasis of harmony and
rhythm. For the balance and symmetry which are
essential to good artistic work are also, he conceived,
essential to true artistic feeling. Love is the typical
feeling awakened by sensuous beauty, and the genuine
love of genuine beauty is incompatible with un-
governed emotion. The mere 'mad' intensity of
animal appetite has nothing to do with such love,
which is not for the body except so far as it is the
expression of soul. 'Where beauty of inward character
meets with beauty of outward form, each correspond-

ing and harmonizing with the other, and cast in a common mould, there is the fairest sight to a man who has the eyes to see it. And what is most fair is also most lovable.' It is this perfect accord of the inward and the outward which the truly 'musical' man seeks and delights in; but if it cannot be realized, if one or the other element must be imperfect, he will surrender the outward, and while no perfection of form will atone to him for defect of soul, he 'will not refuse to take pleasure in' a fair soul even though it appear in an 'inharmonious' body.

Before considering the general view here given of the functions of art in education, a word must be said about the relative position which Plato assigns to the various specific arts. We are at once struck by the great prominence given to music as compared with painting, sculpture, and architecture; and this may seem the more surprising when we remember the excellence attained by the Greeks in the last two and the rudimentary character of their achievements in the first. It may be that Plato did not see in the sculptors and architects of his time the signs of degeneracy which drew his attention to the poets and musicians; but more probably he estimated the practical influence of the former upon the national character as less important than that of the latter. The frame of mind in which pictures and statues, and still more buildings, are most appreciated and enjoyed, is rather one of open and undisturbed receptivity than of active emotion, and to most temperaments the burning word and the stirring melody have far more effect

The position assigned to the different arts

upon action than brilliancy of colouring or majesty of form. But whatever may be the cause, it is a fact worthy of attention that a philosophical iconoclast like Plato, in attacking the idols of sensationalism both in knowledge and morality, should have almost ignored the painters and sculptors, and confined his assaults to the musicians and still more to the poets. Another noticeable point is the simplicity and uniformity of the criteria which Plato applies to the several arts. Proportion, in one form or another, is the single source to which he refers all artistic excellence, in the musical relations of time and tone no less than in those of space in the arts of form and construction. And this leads us lastly to remark how extremely rudimentary must have been the music of which he was speaking. He assumes throughout that music always implies words, and the whole subject of harmony, in its modern sense, is absent from his consideration. The truth seems to be, paradoxical as it may sound, that it was the very simplicity of Greek music which led Greek writers to assign to it such a direct and important educational influence. As in the early days of sculpture or painting, the crudeness and symbolism makes the meaning of the artist more clear, when compared with the subtle design and colouring of great masters, so when music was chiefly limited to an accompaniment giving emphasis or precision to a recitation or a dance, its effect would be more strongly recognized in proportion as it was more simple. Even now there are dancing and marching melodies which exercise a direct and almost physical

influence on a susceptible hearer, just because there
is nothing but the simple act of dancing or marching
which they suggest; and if music generally were
intimately associated with a few elementary acts and
feelings, its power, being more easily expressible,
would be also more reducible to rule and to practice,
than when it has developed into a vast and independent growth, speaking in its own language and obeying
its own laws, of which it is itself the sole interpreter.

This difference, however, great as it is, and much Art and
as it increases the difficulty of applying Plato's ideas character
to modern music, does not except it from the general
scope of his theory concerning the educational use of
art, the main features of which we may now proceed
to consider. Of these the central and most characteristic one is undoubtedly the idea that art may have,
and ought to have, a definite function in the development of character; and we have to ask how Plato
conceived this function to be exercised. 'Education
in music,' he says, 'is so telling, because rhythm and
harmony sink so deeply into the inward part of the
soul, and take hold of it so strongly, and make it
graceful with the grace which they bring with them.'
And again, 'Gracefulness and ungracefulness go along
with rhythmicalness and unrhythmicalness, and
rhythmicalness and unrhythmicalness follow and
resemble goodness of language, or the reverse; the
style of language, again, follows the character of soul,
and thus goodness of language, of harmony, of form,
and of rhythm go along with goodness of character.'
'Are the gestures and accents of a brave soul in trouble

the same as those of a cowardly one?' he asks in a closely analogous passage of the *Laws*; 'surely not; the very colours of the two men are different'. From these few passages, which could easily be multiplied, so much is clear, that Plato was in earnest with the idea that there is some real connexion between

Proportion the essential common element in both

character and artistic form, and that the common element in both is found in the rightness of proportion which is essential alike to beauty in art and to goodness in conduct. We shall perhaps understand him better if we reflect (what the passages above will suggest) that in the early stages of civilization the whole of life tends to be more symbolical, and the connexion between mental states and their physical expression more immediate. In such stages speech has something of the crudity of a language of signs, while gesture and sound approach the delicacy and articulateness of words. With the progress of civilization the symbolism of sense does not, as is sometimes supposed, disappear, but it gets infinitely more complex and subtle; colours and lines, tones and measures, instead of being like letters of an alphabet with fixed and uniform values, become fitful centres of multitudinous associations, so various to different sensibilities, and so remote from their primitive significance, that men are tempted to deny their validity or to relegate them to the sphere of individual caprice. It is curious to see the human mind thus refusing to recognize, or to be recognized by, its own offspring as they grow up. In the infancy of art, nobody doubts but that it has a meaning, that mind speaks to mind in it. Only when it has ceased to lisp and to point, when the simple singer has grown into a 'mighty-mouthed inventor of harmonies', and the sculptor's one poor thought has made way for

> 'The thousand sounds and sights that broke
> In on him at the chisel's stroke',

only then do men begin to question whether what they have created is really their own, and to explain it away by chance, by convention, by mechanics, by anything but mind. Yet this is not really to be wondered at; for as soon as we try to account for any but the simplest effects of art, they escape us, the truth being that 'accounting for' them merely means translating one medium of expression into another and less perfect one. Language and music and painting are all significant, but the significance of one is not convertible with that of another. We cannot listen to the meaning of colour and form, we must see it; we cannot make music speak in words without its ceasing to be music, any more than we can resolve a poem into sound and rhythm without its poetry evaporating. And if the relationship of the arts to one another is so difficult to express, much more so is the relationship of art in general to other modes of human activity. Few people, indeed, can seriously doubt that the character of an imaginative man is ultimately affected by what he habitually sees and hears; or, again, that what one person apprehends as right or expedient, another person may apprehend as beautiful; or, once more, that devotion, similar in effect to that of the saint for the being whom he worships, may be felt by the man of science for the truth which he pursues. But when we have made a few general statements such as these, we are brought to a standstill by the intricacy of the subject and the limitations of our analysis. The fact remains irrefragable that to the vast majority of mankind art and conduct, religion and science, are very different things, with little or nothing in common; and that the attempt to fuse them generally results in sermonizing pictures, rose-water morality, and unctuous sciolism. And as, at most times and for most purposes, it is of more practical importance to realize proximate differences than fundamental unities, the world at large instinctively looks with suspicion upon those who, in trying to see through the ordinary distinctions of life, appear to be removing its ordinary landmarks. No one has insisted more strongly than Plato himself upon the dangers of passing too hastily 'from the many to the one'; but for that very reason we need not be afraid to follow him, when, with the courage of his conviction that reason is one in its essence, he leads us now and again to 'a high rock' from which we may see that it is one also in its manifestations. To Plato the laws of proportion, which are the condition of beauty in art, seemed to betoken the presence of the same mind as is revealed in the immutable order of the universe, and more imperfectly in the moral order of human life. He was very far from identifying or confusing artistic beauty with moral goodness; but, believing, as he did, that the whole physical world is 'the image of its maker, God manifest to sense', he could not but believe that in all things sensible, and therefore in the relations of

Proportion in art, character and the order of the universe

figure, time, and tone, there is a right and a wrong, a good and a bad, according as they do or do not express and obey intelligence. And since bodily movement and sight and hearing are among the most prominent and important of our vital activities, especially in early life, he drew the natural conclusion that it must make a difference to the growth of the human soul and character, how, and upon what occasions, those activities are exercised, and that it is the function of the arts to provide for their exercise in the best way and upon the best objects. It is, in fact, rather the real simplicity than the supposed vagueness of Plato's ideas which makes them embarrassing. The luxuriant development of the arts in modern times, in independence both of one another and of the other elements of human life, makes it difficult to apply to them conceptions formed at a time when they were modest and business-like appendages of religion, war, or public amusement; almost as difficult as it would be to transfer the lessons learnt on a school drilling-ground to the evolutions of a modern army on the battle-field.

Plato would have his young citizens, who are one day to govern and protect the state, nerved and inspirited, soothed and softened, by warlike and peaceful songs; he would have them disciplined to order by the precision of time and tune, of movement and voice; he would remind them of their duties by the sculpturesque embodiments of undying types of true manhood; he would make grace and dignity as natural to them as the air which they breathe, and lead them to bear themselves unconsciously as if they were in the presence of others. In all this there is nothing strange. But from the austere beauty of the conception of the Greek philosopher to the confused jargon of modern aesthetic culture, is a bewildering and unwelcome step. Our masterpieces of art are mostly foreign, and speak a language unintelligible to the ordinary English mind. Even if it were otherwise, they are meaninglessly arranged in galleries, cut adrift from the surroundings for which they were made, but which they can never recover. Our greatest artists are going back to an unreal or unnational past, or 'are making the public their master more than necessity requires'. Where are we to look for the 'breeze of beauty and health', for the craftsmen who 'can track out the nature of loveliness and grace'? We may collect engravings, and photographs, and china, and make ourselves learned in the history of art; we may found museums and institutes, and spread casts of Venus and Apollo through the land; we may give thousands of pounds for pieces of clever vulgarity; but we shall not make English life much more beautiful or more joyous, unless we can produce art which will educate the nation to see with its eyes and to hear with its ears the country in which it dwells and the history which it inherits. It is in music perhaps that the outlook is the least discouraging. Here there is a possibility of acting upon large masses with some effect; here social distinctions are less felt; here too the English nature seems to show more aptitude and susceptibility. We can hardly hope to make our great towns beautiful, but it is not chimerical to look forward to a time when

How far can the principle be realized in modern English life?

they may each have their orchestra and chorus, and adequate provision for hearing them. There is no need to quarrel about the precise educational effect which modern music has or may have. That it has some such effect will not be denied except by those who wish to keep it to themselves, or by those who are irritated at the stupidity of its would-be advocates. The apparent vagueness of its influence, arising from the difficulty of formulating it, is neither a proof of its unreality nor an argument against utilizing it. Everybody who is at all susceptible to music knows that he is better for having it, and worse for being without it; he also probably knows that the composers whom the world has agreed to call great are, some, or all of them, those to whose music he most likes to listen; more than this he need not be able to say, for a fact is not made more of a fact by being talked or written about. If it be once fully recognized that music has a great emotional power over a considerable proportion of English people, the proper application of the power becomes a public duty, and it is only a question of time to discover the best ways of doing it.

We have thus far considered Plato's conception of the education in 'music', mainly in its ethical and psychological aspect, but we should represent him very imperfectly if we omitted to mention the importance which he attaches to it on social and political grounds. The often-quoted text, that 'the fashions of music are never changed without changes in the most important laws of the commonwealth', may serve here as a point of departure. It is difficult for us to under-

'Music' and political life

stand the concern with which Plato urges the importance of permanence and continuity in the system of 'musical' education. 'It is in music', he says, 'that the guardians of our state must build their guardhouse; for it is here that lawlessness easily creeps in unperceived. People think that it is only play, and does no harm. And what harm does it do? Little by little it gets a footing, and spreads gently and silently into the habits and arrangements of life; from these it passes, gathering force as it goes, into the transactions of business, and from business it gets to the laws and the constitution, with licence full-grown in its train, until it ends by ruining everything, both public and private.' On the other hand, 'when the play of children is good from the first, and they take in a spirit of law through their music, then it has just the opposite effect, attending them at every step in life, making it grow, and building it up where it had fallen down'. And as in the other case the spirit of lawlessness, beginning at the trifles of education, ends by overthrowing law itself, so the law-loving temper, fostered from childhood, is the pregnant germ of the full insight of the legislator and statesman. If it only be started well, it will assimilate nourishment and grow by its own inherent vitality. To people who have thus lived in an atmosphere of order, the details of legislation will offer no difficulty; with an instinctive and inherited tact they will regulate their life wisely and well, whether it be in the lesser matters of social behaviour and usage, or in the greater ones of business, commerce, and trade.

We have had occasion before to remark on the difference between the small and simple civic communities of Greece and the complex masses of modern nations, in regard to the directness and rapidity of the transmission of social and political changes. The passage just quoted brings that difference again vividly before us. To Plato, with the restlessness and instability of Greek political life before his eyes, the one thing needful seemed to be to establish in society a permanent 'ethos', a traditional character, which should be able to resist the shocks of party-spirit and individual caprice. And if this could only be done by a system of education, which should receive each citizen at birth and retain its hold upon him through life, it was no mere fancy to watch with a jealous eye the first symptoms of innovation in the system, even in matters so apparently trivial as popular songs. To us, with our national gift for forming and carrying on traditional modes of life and thought, it will often seem that in education we need more exhortation to adopt new ideas than to remain faithful to old ones. Our great schools and universities are typical instances of the way in which prejudice and tradition may uphold methods of teaching and social habits which have ceased to have a reason for existence. As regards the other part of Plato's opinion, that for men who are going to serve their country in government and legislation the early formation of a 'constitutional' character is of much more importance than a study of written systems or codes, we are more nearly at one with him. If the Duke of Wellington could say that the battle of

Waterloo was won on the playing-fields at Eton, we need not be surprised at Plato when he speaks of children 'receiving the spirit of law through their music', or when he says that 'one of the greatest tests of a man's character is the show which he makes in his gymnastics'. The distrust in 'technical' education for the higher spheres of public life, and the belief in the efficacy of a 'liberal culture', which glories in having nothing directly to do with a profession, are both strong, sometimes perhaps too strong, in the English mind. Even if the theory itself were in no danger of being overdriven, the poverty of the culture which we provide on the strength of it might give us some qualms. The principle of our system, put at its best, is that by taking the mind through the greatest works of classical literature, we both train it to habits of exactitude and observation, and cultivate the taste, imagination, and judgement with the finest and wisest thought of antiquity. We inherit the system from an age when the language and literature of modern Europe had only just begun to exist, and when great thoughts adequately expressed could only be found in classical writers. The value of the intellectual discipline gained in the curriculum cannot seriously be disputed; but whether, as it is at present worked, even when supplemented by the teaching of parts of the Bible, it supplies the best and most natural food to the 'philosophic' element in the English mind, is extremely doubtful. It is not indeed upon this ground, of inadequacy for its professed purpose, that the system is generally attacked; its assailants are more

The theory and practice of a liberal education in England

often persons who are crying out for 'practical' education, and who, if they had their way, would eliminate from the culture of the human mind the study of its own greatest works. But it is just this which makes the question a serious one. For if the position of the higher education is assailed from without by misguided or mercenary ignorance, while its natural defenders are beginning to doubt whether they have anything to defend, we may well fear for its future. In the confusion and din which surrounds the subject, nothing seems so important as to come to a clear understanding of the point at issue. It should be seen that convenient catchwords like 'supply' and 'demand', or well-sounding oppositions like 'words' and 'things', tell us absolutely nothing unless we realize first by what the 'demand' is made, and what 'things' are. It should be understood that the primary question is, not whether to refine the taste, or to produce a gentleman, or to teach useful knowledge, is the end of education; but, before all, how the whole man is to be made the best of; and that whether it be nature and her works, or man and his works which are studied (and neither can be rightly neglected), it is ultimately mind in some form or another which we have to educate, and mind in some form or another through which alone it can be educated. The representatives of religion, literature, and science might then join hands over their common subject-matter, instead of snatching at it by turns, and trying each to undo the work of his supposed rival. In the meantime, until we are nearer to such a result, two lesser and more practicable things may be done by the teachers of language; they may try to make classical education less a matter of mere grammatical discipline or of imitative ingenuity, and more a study of human thought and character; and they may try to rescue our own English literature from its present neglect, to treat it in the spirit of the great men who have created scholarship, not on methods combining the worst features of the traditional classical curriculum, and, by making it speak to the youth of the nation, give it a systematic place in the development of the national character.

What will happen if we neglect education in 'music'?

We may conclude Plato's representation of the political and social importance of 'musical' education by looking with him for a moment at some of the consequences of its neglect. In the eighth and ninth books of the *Republic*, Plato has given us in a series of pictures an ideal history of the fall of the human soul, both in the individual and in society. He had previously shown us what he conceived that the life of man might be if it were allowed to follow the highest law of its development; he now shows us to what lowest depths it might be supposed to sink if the logical principle of degeneration were allowed to work unchecked. He had followed man up to the point at which he is nearest to God; he now traces his descent to the point when he is on the verge of passing into a beast. In this picture of the progress of evil a strikingly prominent place is assigned to the gradually increasing neglect of 'music'; and nowhere does Plato express more clearly his sense of the vital importance, social and political, of a thing apparently so far removed from society and politics as the early culture of the higher side of human nature. The ideally best condition of life, individual and social, had been represented by him as resulting from the harmonious and normal development and operation of certain psychical forces. In accordance with this view, the gradual declension from such a condition is represented as a continually increasing discord in the vital faculties, beginning with the failure of the highest to perform their proper functions, and the usurpation of their place by lower ones, and ending with the complete inversion of the true psychological relations, and the absolute dominion of those activities which have no right even to exist in the organism. And as the ideally best conditions were conceived by Plato to depend upon a right system of education, maintaining and transmitting a certain character, so the typical forms of evil or imperfection in the world are pictured by him as resulting from the abandonment or perversion of such a system, the soul being thereby deprived of its proper nourishment, and left a victim to the bad influences of its environment and its own lower nature.

The first effect of the neglect of 'music' is a certain loss of elevation in the general aim of life. The 'philosophic' faculties, deprived of their true object, find exercise in calculating means to lower ends, and in this unnatural service lose that simplicity and directness which are alone compatible with the pursuit of truth in the interests of society. The element of 'spirit' rises into the place thus left vacant, and makes the desire for distinction the ruling principle of life. But the falseness of its position reacts upon it; deprived of the higher inspiration which its nature requires, Stages and ways of decline it sinks itself into mere personal ambition, while the meaner desires, which it should have joined with reason to regulate or repress, begin to lift up their heads. Such is Plato's psychological diagnosis of certain well-known social phenomena. When the best intellects in the community begin to be suspected of being 'too clever', and are kept out of high places in favour of 'honest and downright' men; when self-respect tends to degenerate into self-will, and the desire for personal distinction becomes a passion; when moral rectitude is upheld more by fear of disgrace than by inward conviction, and a chivalrous bearing in public is compatible with the pursuit of money and pleasure 'in the dark'; then we may suspect that 'the Muses are beginning to be neglected', and that 'reason tempered with music, which is the only guardian-angel of virtue', is being driven from its natural home in the souls of men.

The continued neglect of education brings with it more aggravated results. As the eye of the mind grows more and more unaccustomed to the vision of beauty and truth, its sight gets more and more narrowed to the objects nearest to it, and the 'blind god' of wealth becomes the leader of the 'blind' soul. And the fresh downward step of the higher self is accompanied by a fresh rise in the lower; the animal appetites, which ambition had affected to despise and repress, now no longer 'tamed' by reason or swayed by high purpose, become noisy and importunate; and though respectability and self-interest may still keep them down, 'want of education' leaves them free to engender a brood of 'drone-like' passions, unproductive and inorganic, the paupers and criminals of the soul. The same 'want of education', operating over a wider area, produces analogous conditions in a state, where the neglected and unnurtured children of the upper classes first sink into unproductive spendthrifts, and then swell the useless and dangerous elements of the society which, in its blind devotion to money, had helped to impoverish them.

It is a further stage in decline when the comparative respectability and consistency of the pursuit of wealth gives way to the mere restlessness of indiscriminate impulse, and the satisfaction of the passing moment is erected into a principle of life. Here, again, it is the 'uneducated' soul which falls a victim. A father, who believes in nothing that does not pay, gives his son a cheap education. The son gets into fast society; its flashiness dazzles his eyes, which have never learnt to look at anything but the ground; after a struggle perhaps he temporarily recovers his hereditary steadiness, but his soul is still empty and barren, and weeds, both native and exotic, have full liberty to grow there. The 'words of truth and beauty, which are the best garrison of souls whom God loves', have never been allowed to hold their rightful citadel, and their vacant place is gradually occupied by the 'false and swaggering' theories, which promise 'initiation' into the 'mysterious' knowledge of the world. Their key to the mystery is simple, and consists in 'calling insolence good breeding, anarchy freedom, prodigality magnificence, and shamelessness manhood'. For a soul so circumstanced, the best chance is that it may stop in its career of licence before it has become the victim of any one dominant passion, and arrive at a sort of equilibrium in its desires, satisfying them each in turn, and living that life of so-called 'freedom' which consists in being the creature of the moment. But if circumstances are not so favourable to it, the trembling balance of discordant appetites is sure to be overset, the irresistible impulse of passion to absorb everything unless it be itself absorbed will assert itself, and the easy-going 'liberty and equality' of many-coloured caprice will settle down into the cruel and sombre 'tyranny' of lust.

The ruin of the soul

These meagre fragments, from what forms perhaps the most powerfully written section of the *Republic*, will suffice to illustrate Plato's conception of the consequences of neglecting the education of the reason through the imagination and the emotions. They will show how strongly he felt the truth which we are sometimes in danger of forgetting, that the evil in human life is quite as much due to negative as to positive conditions; that it is the absence of healthy and bright surroundings, the want of healthy and interesting employments, the abeyance of healthy and inspiring emotions, which drag so many men down. We cannot help seeing this in the case of the lower strata of society, where the pressure of circumstances is so gross and palpable; but if we agree with Plato, we shall feel that the more richly endowed and the more delicately organized human nature is, the more important and also the more difficult it is to educate it well, and the more fatal are the consequences, both to itself and to society, of educating it badly or not at all. And what is true of different natures compared with one another, is true also of the different elements in the same nature. Good, like evil, begins at the top and radiates downwards. If we can secure that the highest faculties, intellectual and emotional, are at their highest activity, the lower ones will not probably be seriously disorganized; but no amount of decent regularity in the working of the lower will guarantee the vitality of the higher. 'When the whole soul follows the philosophic element, and there is no faction in it, the justice of each separate part is secured, and each does its own work and reaps its own pleasures too, the best pleasures, and also up to its measure the truest. But when any of the other elements dominates, it not only fails to find its own pleasure itself, but it compels the other elements to pursue a pleasure which is not their own nor true.'

The evils arising from the neglect of 'music' are not the only evils which Plato describes in connexion with it; we have already seen what he considered to be the psychological effects of its excessive or exclusive study. To obviate these effects is, as we also saw, the proper function of gymnastic; and we have now to complete our account of Plato's conception of that branch of education. Of this, as of music, he only lays down certain general 'outlines' or principles, leaving the details to be filled in by those who have to apply them.

The second discipline in the elementary stage: Gymnastic

The most important of these principles, which we have already had occasion to notice, is that gymnastic, though concerned primarily with the body, is to be *Primarily* considered as ultimately affecting the soul and the *concerned* *with the* character, and owes to this fact its educational im- *body, but* *ultimately* portance. This principle at once determines the *affecting* *the soul* general aim of bodily exercises; they should aim 'not so much at producing mere strength, as at awakening the spirited element in human nature'. It is the fault of the professional trainers that they ignore the educational side of their business, and attend only to developing the muscles. And their system not only fails in an ethical point of view, but even where it might be expected to succeed, it does not really do so. 'The athletic habit of body is a sleepy sort of habit, and is liable to upset the health. We see how the professional athletes doze away their life, and how, if they deviate a little from their prescribed diet, they get serious and violent diseases.' A 'finer kind of training' is wanted for a man who is to serve his country as a soldier; he must have his wits awake, be quick of sight and hearing, and able to endure changes of food and weather without breaking down. Of the two elements in such a training, diet and exercise, Plato, in the *Republic*, devotes much more consideration to the former. The most characteristic point in what he says of the latter is, that for a certain period physical exercise should be pursued alone, to the exclusion of all serious mental work. This period would apparently be from two to three years, between the ages of seventeen and twenty. Two reasons are given for this view: that 'hard work and sleep are enemies to study', and that 'the figure which a man makes in his gymnastic is one of the greatest tests of his character'. Every one who knows anything of English school life Exercise will be ready to endorse both these statements; but he will not probably consider the truth of them a reason for making two years and a half of exclusive athletic exercises a necessary part of education. We must remember, however, that Plato was thinking of something more analogous to an incipient military service than to the games of our schools. The exercises upon which so long a time was to be spent would aim principally at disciplining the body for the work of a soldier, and would include, if practicable, some actual 'taste of blood' on the battle-field. Still, even with this explanation, it is curious that his belief in the importance of 'specializing' work should have so far overruled his consciousness of the dangers of one-sided development.

Plato has more to say on the other branch of gym- Diet nastic, the system of diet and general management of the body; for he is here brought into contact with the medical practice of his day, and about this he held some strong opinions. Impressed with the want of principle and purpose, of simplicity and concentration, in all departments of Greek life, he saw in the recent growth of luxury, with its attendant crop of new diseases, and its new methods of medical treatment, an analogous phenomenon to that which he observed in the sphere of art. While the artists seemed to him to be mainly engaged in catering for a morbid appetite for emotional stimulants, helping to enervate

4166 N

morality and to fill the law-courts with litigants, instead of to make men a law to themselves, the doctors, he thought, were pampering a luxurious valetudinarianism, and flattering the whims of rich voluptuaries whose disorders were the result of their own mismanagement. The simplicity for which he had cried aloud in art, he now demanded in living, and upon the same grounds. In a well-ordered society every man ought to have his work to do; and if he has work to do, he must make himself fit to do it. The spiced luxuries of a feverish civilization, with its 'sauces from Sicily', its 'grisettes from Corinth', its 'Athenian confectionery', have no more place in his life than they would have if he were training for a race. Most of the long names which recent medicine has given to diseases are, in Plato's opinion, the polite inventions of doctors who will not offend their rich patients by telling them the truth, that they have worked too little and eaten too much. A man who is always wanting to see a physician, except in case of accidents or epidemics, ought to be as much ashamed of himself as a man who is always going into court to get justice, because he has none of his own. We might learn a lesson here from the despised artisan. He cannot afford to be long in bed; his work will not wait for him; and if he cannot be cured soon, he dies. But the rich man is supposed to have no work to do, abstention from which would make life not worth living. He is to be allowed to give up his duties as a householder or a citizen, or to let his brain lie fallow as long as he likes, whenever he fancies that he has a sick headache.

Modern life would have supplied Plato with close analogies to the evils which he saw in the gymnastics and dietetics of his own day. Our public schools and universities have no lack of the sleepy and brutalized athlete, who has not an idea of doing anything except by force, whose perceptions are cloyed and dull, whose 'life moves without grace or rhythm', and who yet probably could not serve on a campaign or a geographical expedition. Nor is the well-to-do valetudinarian an unfamiliar creature amongst us, the man who 'suffers torments if he depart at all from his accustomed diet', and 'is always in labour about his body'. Both phenomena may be said to represent the bad sides of something which is intrinsically good; the exaggerated interest taken in athletic exercises, while it partly defeats its own aim by artificializing school life, and making games into professions, is nevertheless the outcome of a genuine desire to broaden the basis of education, and to lose no chance of developing character out of strong national tendencies. So, too, the attention given to diet and the less serious forms of ailment, though it may sometimes result in making a man 'profitable neither to himself or society', is a symptom of the higher and more intelligent value which is set upon human life. Every real advance in civilization, along with the higher responsibilities and the more delicate public conscience which it brings with it, entails also fresh forms of abuse and greater necessity for taking trouble; but the best modern minds will not agree with Plato that it is the duty of society to let anybody die who can be kept alive. If,

however, we have advanced upon his ideas in this
point, we are still far from having realized them in
others. We have not yet found the best way 'to blend
music with gymnastic and apply them proportionately
to the soul' of the average schoolboy; and we have
scarcely begun to entertain the idea that a man is as
much bound to manage his health properly as he is
to manage his morals, much less to diffuse the knowledge which would enable him to do it.

Let us now gather up briefly the main threads in
Recapitu- Plato's account of 'musical' education, which, in its
lation
wider sense, as implying the harmonious development
of the whole nature, includes 'gymnastic' as well as
'music'. Its function is to provide nurture for the soul
from childhood to youth. Upon the lower or 'appetitive' element its action is more indirect than direct;
it tames, regulates, or represses its various manifestations, by encouraging interests and emotions by which
they are absorbed, or with which they are incompatible, as the case may require. Upon the 'spirited'
and 'philosophic' elements it acts directly, by compelling and encouraging their normal activity through
the bodily limbs and senses. The means which it
employs for the former are diet and exercise, for the
latter they are poetry and the arts. These last are the
appropriate nurture of the 'philosophic' nature, not in
its entirety, but in that phase of its growth in which it
is mainly imaginative and emotional, not logical and
reflective. By presenting to the soul the true principles
of human life in the sensuous material which it is
able to assimilate, they prepare it unconsciously for

assimilating them when presented at a later stage in a more rational form. They teach it how to live by telling how divine beings and great men live and have lived; they teach it what to love by surrounding it with what is really lovable; they foster its acquisitive instincts by encouraging the quick and accurate use of the senses; they develop its tendency to order and law by accustoming it to recognize severe symmetries of sound and form; and, finally, they introduce it to manhood endowed with an instinctive capacity of doing and saying the right thing at the right time, and with an instinctive perception of what is right and wrong in the deeds and words of others. In calling the capacity and perception thus acquired 'instinctive', it is not intended that Plato conceived them to be received at birth or got by natural selection. No doubt Plato did attach immense importance to natural endowment; no doubt also he believed that there was some natural tendency in human nature towards what was good for it; but we have abundantly seen that this belief was more than counterbalanced by a conviction that mere natural endowment may be simply destructive, and that a mere tendency to what is good may ultimately tend to what is bad. By 'instinctive' then is meant that the substance of the education of 'music' is appropriated and held by the soul without real reflection; that, in Greek phraseology, it feels neither the need nor the capacity to 'give an account of' it; that it is conscious of it only as part and parcel of itself, not as an object which it can hold apart, look at, and criticize. Such a condition of mind is not of course unreflective in the sense of implying any capriciousness or instability; on the contrary, the imperceptible degrees by which it has been formed guarantee its depth and fixity. And, accordingly, when Plato wishes to describe finally the effects of 'music' upon the character, he can find no better metaphor than one taken from the process of dyeing. The dyers, he says, when they want to dye wool a fine purple, first select white wool from amongst the various colours; then they prepare it very carefully to receive the bloom, and then at last they dye it; a dye put in in this way is fast for ever, whereas if otherwise treated it washes out in a ridiculous manner. 'This then was what we were trying to do when we selected our citizen-soldiers and educated them by music and gymnastic; our whole object was that by obedience they should take in the laws like a dye so that their belief about danger and all other things might become fast, through their having both the proper nature and the proper nurture, and thus the influences of pleasure, pain, fear, and appetite, which are more potent than all the soaps and solvents in the world, might never be able to wash it out.'

The dyeing of the soul

IV. THE HIGHER STUDIES AND THE ASCENT TO TRUTH

Something more is required The question now arises, Is education so conceived complete? Is the soul, when nurtured up to this point, full-grown as far as education can make it? At one time Plato seems to have thought that it was; that at about twenty a man must cease learning in the narrower sense of the word, and get the rest of his knowledge in the practical life of a citizen, and that it rested with those in authority to watch his development and regulate his career accordingly. But we have also seen that in the second section of the *Republic*, he clearly expresses his feeling of the imperfection of the education of 'music', and assigns to it a subordinate and preparatory function in a more elaborate system. There are two main points in which Plato finds it imperfect: subjectively, from the side of the soul, it leaves important capacities undeveloped; objectively, regarding the matter which it imparts and the form in which it imparts it, it stops short of the requirements of knowledge. On the one hand, it teaches the 'philosophic' nature to love what is beautiful, but not to understand what is true; it makes it quick to recognize the forms of goodness presented to sense or imagination, but not to see with the mind's eye the essential principles which those forms imperfectly express; it infuses into it indelible beliefs and convictions, attaching to the particular characters and actions which have come before it in the course of education, but it does not satisfy the desire to know the laws to which those beliefs can be referred. On the other hand, if we regard the matter which it teaches, this consists mainly of ideas embodied in sensible forms; the characters and deeds of individual men are described in poetry or suggested in music or pictured in painting and sculpture, with the view of stimulating imitation and educating the sense for the corresponding realities

The soul has further capacities to be developed: and there is more to know

in life. The ideas thus imparted carry conviction to the soul, not through their logical consistency and irrefragability, but through their familiarity; they are apprehended, not in the systematic form of science in which each part is seen to be connected with every other, but as a multitude of isolated instances, each complete in itself, and containing its own justification. A person in this mental condition does not satisfy the requirements of what Plato understands by knowledge; and here few thoughtful people would disagree with him; where he differs from most of the world is in thinking that the further mental progress, instead of being left to the circumstances and choice of the individual, should be systematically provided for by a continued education. He seems to have been led to this idea by reflecting upon the consequences which seemed to him to follow from the neglect of it. He was persuaded that the evils of human life had their root in ignorance, and that if men could once realize what their true interests required them to do, they would do it. He did not expect that mankind at large should ever have such a keen and profound perception of the truth, but it seemed to him not impossible that a few exceptional persons might arrive at it, and that society might allow itself to be governed by them; at any rate he was convinced that this sovereignty of true knowledge was the ideal to be aimed at, convinced that there is an intelligible principle pervading and connecting not only the life of men but the life of the whole universe, convinced that to discern this principle and to conform to it is the highest achievement of knowledge and of conduct, and that to 'rise by stepping-stones' towards this height is the true education both of the individual and of the human race. Of such a principle the education of 'music' had nothing to tell; it showed examples and types of courage, temperance, justice, but it did not show 'wherein they are good', what is the end to which they all converge, and which gives unity and meaning to their variety; and without some such perception how can we be said to 'know' justice, or even to possess it? We may know it in one form, but we might mistake it in another; we may think we have got hold of it at one moment, in one place, under one set of circumstances, but it may escape us when we have changed our point of view. This is why the results of the first education are 'sketchy' and 'inexact', and require 'filling up' and completing by a further education.

But there was another consideration which led Plato to the same conclusion. It has already been shown how the conception of what he called the 'philosophic' nature grows under his hands in the *Republic*, and how from being a complementary psychological element it comes ultimately to be represented as the germ of complete manhood. *And there is a danger that without further training the great natures, the 'philosophic' natures, may be corrupted* Though, however, it has in it this inherent capability, like other germs it depends for its development upon its environment, and Plato is the first to admit, and even to insist upon, the fact, that this richly endowed 'philosophic' nature, which might be the cause of the greatest good to mankind, is generally the cause of the greatest evils. The reason of this strange phenomenon is found, partly in the very gifts of the nature itself, partly in the external advantages, so called, which it usually commands. Driven by the native force of genius, it cannot rest in the narrow conventionalities of common opinion. But its unquenchable thirst for what is real, its far-reaching vision, its magnificent aspirations, find no true satisfaction or guidance. The atmosphere in which it lives is public opinion, speaking through its hired mouthpieces, who think themselves its leaders; loud, exaggerated, irresistible, intolerant of principles, and confident in facts, which are really nothing but the dictates of its own caprice. What can save a great nature in such an atmosphere, especially if his force of mind be supplemented by beauty and strength, wealth and connexions? His power is flattered by venal servility, his ambition spoiled by easy triumphs; he feels the world within his grasp. And if some wiser man whisper in his ear the hard truth that he is living the life of a fool, how should he listen? Or if his better genius chance to make him listen, how should he escape the clutches of the parasites, who had looked forward to living upon his success? So it is that the philosophic nature is corrupted, and sinks to a life unworthy of itself, while philosophy, deserted by her true kinsmen, falls a victim to any jackanapes who can afford to despise his own profession, and bears in this enforced and unnatural union the wretched bastards who go about the world bearing her name, and bringing shame upon their mother. Only here and there, by some exceptional circumstance, ill health perhaps, or banishment, or pride, or possibly an inward and inexplicable monition, a man of the true stuff is kept back from public life and saved for philosophy; and those poor few can do nothing better than stand aside out of the storm of the world, happy if they can live without sin and die in hope. Such is Plato's indictment against the society in which he was living. 'No one of the forms of constitution now existing is worthy of the philosophic nature. Therefore it is changed and distorted, and as a seed sown in a strange soil will lose its virtue and become a victim to the influences amongst which it lives, so in the present state of things this kind of soul does not keep its force, but falls away to a nature not its own. But if it can find a form of society good enough for it, then men will see that it was always really divine, and that all else in their nature and ways of life is human only.'

It is then in the interests of society, whether we regard them as endangered by want of real knowledge, or by the neglect and corruption of its noblest natures, that Plato finds a further education to be necessary; and the question is, firstly, How did he conceive of the higher kind of apprehension which he called knowledge and the higher form of object which he called truth, and by what means did he think that the mind might be educated to the knowledge of such truth? and secondly, How did he hope to avoid the dangers attendant on the philosophic nature, and to make it an instrument of salvation instead of destruction to society? These two questions were to Plato really one; for in his view the dominant impulse of

What did he mean by knowledge and truth?

the philosophic nature is the impulse to know the truth, and to know the truth of things is to know the reason of them and to know their reason completely would be to see them as convergent parts in a whole governed by a single end, or, in Platonic language, a single 'good'; so that ultimately to know the truth of the world would be to know 'the good' of the world, or the 'reason why' of its existence, and to understand human life thoroughly would be to see the end or purpose which governs it in the light of that larger end or purpose which makes the whole universe luminous and intelligible. Thus the true interests of society coincide with those of its highest natures; for the study of what the good of man is and requires, is the best way of satisfying the best impulse of those natures, and the same process which develops the philosophic mind to its highest pitch, and makes a man a true philosopher, will bring it also to the knowledge of the principles which should guide human conduct, and will make a man a true statesman. Thus the question with Plato comes to be, What is the education by which the human mind may be brought nearer to that truth which is at once the keystone of knowledge and the pole star of conduct? And this question is most instructively treated under three heads, firstly, What is the nature of intellectual progress? the answer to which will give us a scale of knowledge and truth up which education should lead the mind; secondly, What is the nature and cause of human ignorance, which keeps the mind from thus advancing? and thirdly, What are the specific means

There is a truth which is at once the keystone of knowledge, and the pole-star of conduct and government

by which this ignorance may be removed, and the How can
we attain
inherent capacity of the mind developed and regu- it?
lated? The last only of these questions concerns
education directly; but just as in the case of the earlier
education of character it was impossible to understand Plato without considering the constituent elements out of which the character had to be formed,
so in order to make intelligible his account of the
later education of reason, it is indispensable to consider in a general way how he conceived the activity
and sphere of reason, in other words, knowledge and
truth. And further, as Plato's manner of developing
a view by antagonism to an existing state of things is
nowhere more forcibly illustrated than in his treatment of this part of his subject, we should be throwing
away the half of our information if, in examining the
ideal of knowledge at which he aimed, we neglected
his picture of the ignorance from which he wished to
escape.

At the end of the sixth book of the *Republic* Plato The nature
of intel-
gives us, under the figure of a line divided into four lectual
progress
parts, a series of the objects of mental apprehension,
and of the mental operations which correspond to
them, arranged in an ascending order of clearness
and truth. At the bottom of the scale of objects he
places what he calls 'images', and at the bottom of the
scale of mental activities the 'perception of images'.
By 'images' he understands primarily shadows and
reflections, but he seems also to include under the
term any perceivable object which reproduces or
suggests another in the same kind of way that shadows

and reflections suggest and reproduce the things which occasion them. Thus all works of art may be called, more or less appropriately, 'images', for it is common to them all to represent how things appear, or what they suggest to sense or imagination, by means of words, sound, colour, or form, which, however directly related to the things, cannot be identified with them. This is of course far from being a full account of what the arts do; but they all do at least this, and Plato, for reasons which we shall presently see, chose to emphasize this characteristic of artistic representation, and to class together indiscriminately all objects of perception to which it is common. Judged then by the standard of clearness and truth, the lowest kind of perception is that which perceives merely shadows, reflections, or analogous images, of things, whatever the medium through which the image is conveyed. The Greek substantive (εἰκασία) used by Plato to describe this 'perception of images', means literally the act of making one thing like another. The corresponding verb, besides the corresponding sense of copying or imitating, is commonly used in the sense of 'conjecturing', apparently because one of the most obvious forms of conjecture is an inference drawn from comparing, that is, mentally 'making like', one thing to another. No doubt this double association of the verb recommended the substantive to Plato's use; for it enabled him conveniently to characterize the lowest stage of perception, not merely as a perception of 'images', but also as having only a 'conjectural' certitude. It is obvious that if we

From the perception of 'images'

compare the knowledge about an object or an event derived from a picture or a description, with the knowledge of a person who has seen the object or been present at the event, the former is not only more indirect and superficial than the latter, but the certainty which we are justified in feeling about it is also less.

It would seem to be in relation to the last-mentioned sense of εἰκασία that Plato calls the next stage in the scale of knowledge πίστις, 'belief' or 'conviction'. Here, as in the former case, when the word has so many associations, it is important to seize the particular one which Plato apparently intended to convey. The objects of 'belief', he says, are the things of which the images of the first stage are resemblances, in other words, what are ordinarily understood by 'real things'. The differences in the mental state of a man whose knowledge consists in 'images' and that of one whose knowledge is derived from personal contact are many, but the one which is emphasized by Plato for his present purpose is that the latter, besides being more clear and true, is also more certain. *to 'belief'*

The two kinds of mental objects and operations just described, while they differ from one another in important respects, have certain other important points in common when both are compared with a higher stage of knowledge; and they are accordingly comprised by Plato under the single generic name of δόξα, or, as it is usually translated, 'opinion'. Neither the Greek word nor its English equivalent, in their ordinary usage, gives any indication of the special meaning which Plato here intended to express. The *We may give the name 'opinion' to both operations* characteristic marks of what he chooses to call 'opinion' are the following: subjectively, it is a state of mind which carries with it no guarantee either of truth or permanence; it may be either true or false (whereas what we understand by 'knowledge' must be true), and it is liable to be changed or lost (whereas when we really know a truth once we know it always); objectively, it relates to a matter which is given in forms of sense, and which is manifold, particular, and relative. An illustration will best explain Plato's meaning. A man has 'opinion' about justice or beauty or weight or size; that is, he 'thinks' that certain things are just or beautiful, heavy or large. His thought may be more or less positive according to his nature and circumstances, but however positive he may feel, he cannot use 'thinking' as equivalent to 'knowing'. If asked, What is justice? What is heaviness? he will probably answer by pointing to this or that instance of what he means: justice perhaps will be to him bound up with certain particular laws, actions, or persons; heaviness with certain particular materials. The respective aggregates of these particular instances will make up his conceptions; justice *is* to him this aggregate, and nothing more. But now, suppose the actions or institutions in which his conception of justice was embodied to be done under different circumstances or worked under different conditions, they may very likely appear to be unjust instead of just. And similarly the materials with which alone he associated heaviness will seem light and not heavy when put alongside of materials which are heavier.

Neither can in any sense be called knowledge

The matter of 'opinion', then, whether it be moral or aesthetic, mathematical or physical (for in this respect there is no difference), is, firstly, 'manifold', consisting of a number of sensible or imaginable objects; and secondly, it is 'particular' and 'relative', for each of its constituents depends for its character upon its own particular position, and changes its character as its relative position changes. And it is clear that these characteristics belong equally to the matter in question, whether it be apprehended directly in actual sensible experience, or indirectly through an artistic or other medium. The condition of mind thus characterized is that of the majority of people on most subjects, and of all people on many subjects. What we commonly call our knowledge, except where we may have made a special study in a special direction, is either derived from the representation of other men, or from our own casual and limited observation of the particular objects with which we happen to have come in contact. On the other hand, though the mind is for the most part content to remain in this condition, there are occasions on which it is conscious of its unsatisfactoriness. This must be the case, for instance, as soon as it begins to see that the sensible qualities of things, which it supposed to be fixed and absolute, are after all variable and relative, and that the same thing seems to have opposite attributes according as its position is changed. This relativity, which is inherent in the matter of sensation, whether in the physical or moral world, is one of the first difficulties which stimulates thought or reflection. The same thing seems to be both light

P

and heavy, both just and unjust; how can this be? Are then lightness and heaviness, justice and injustice, one and the same? To suppose this is to give the lie to one's own consciousness. The dilemma forces the mind to advance and to analyse further this perplexing matter of sensation, which, instead of the clear and permanent thing which it seemed to be, has become a 'confused' centre of contradictory and fluctuating attributes. To detect distinctions in this confusion, to ask, What then really *is* weight? What then really *is* justice? and to distinguish finally the object of sense, with its capacity of developing contradictions and of 'playing double', from the object of thought which can be fixed and defined, these are the further steps which reflection takes, and with these we have left the domain of 'opinion' and entered upon that of science. And this brings us to the next stage in the Platonic scale of mental objects and activities.

Further analysis is needed to disclose the true nature of things

When we reflect upon the meaning of 'knowledge' or 'science' (for the Greek word is the same for both), it seems incongruous to apply it to a state of mind which is liable to error, or to an object-matter which is liable to change. We cannot say that we 'know' what justice is, if the embodiments of our conception may become unjust by a change of relations, any more than we could say that we 'knew' what a triangle was, supposing that we found that the properties of triangles as such varied with the size, colour, or position of the particular figures of which we demonstrated them. This, however, is just what we do not find; we conceive that a triangle is always and everywhere a triangle,

that once known it is always known: and in this belief
we speak of geometrical science or knowledge, which
we distinguish from our ordinary state of mind on
ordinary subjects. What we only 'think' or 'believe'
is scattered about in a number of separate objects;
what we 'know' is one, and only one, however many
may be the instances in which we perceive its truth.
What we only 'think', depends for its character or
validity upon its particular form or environment, and
changes with them; what we 'know' is independent
of its particular presentation, and remains true under
all apparent changes. The state of mind thus distin- The real
guished from 'opinion' is what is commonly under- object of
stood by 'scientific', and as the only sciences which ledge' as
could be said to exist in Plato's time were mathe- from
matical, he took mathematics as the type of the third 'opinion'
stage in his scale of knowledge, though his characteri-
zation of them would equally apply to all sciences
ordinarily so called. The geometrician, Plato says,
uses sensible figures in his reasoning, but does not
really think of them. What he really has in his thought
is not the particular triangle which he draws on paper,
but the 'triangle itself', which the one on paper
'is like' or 'is an image of'. Similarly we might say
of the botanist or political economist, that in proportion as their subject-matter has reached a scientific
stage, they ignore the particular modifications under
which it is presented to them, and see through these
to the essential forms or laws of which they are symbols.
In doing this they have no more doubt than has the
geometrician, that they are nearer to the truth than

if they allowed themselves to attend to nothing but the particular circumstances of the place or the moment. Whatever popular prejudices may be violated by the scientific mode of thought, and whatever metaphysical difficulties may be raised by the assumption of degrees of reality, the best minds are practically, if not theoretically, convinced that there is a difference between 'thinking' and 'knowing', and that in the latter they are more in conformity with what is real than in the former.

The word διάνοια, which Plato appropriated to the form of mental activity just described, had no more fixed connotation in ordinary Greek usage than such English words as 'thought', 'intellect', 'understanding'. We have seen what was the particular meaning which he wished to convey by it, namely, that the next step in the scale of clearness and truth above the mere certainty of opinion, is that in which the mind, while employing sensible objects, is really occupied with something of which they are only symbols or images. It is necessary to dwell at a little more length upon Plato's conception of the distinction here involved, which plays such a vital part in his theory of education and knowledge. The opposition between sense and thought in various forms had attracted the attention of Greek thinkers from the earliest times. The apparent arbitrariness and fluctuation, both of our physical sensations and of our moral ideas, were continually contrasting themselves with the fixity and substantiality which the simplest conception of knowledge and the most rudimentary moral distinc-

Third stage: 'understanding', i.e. the detection by means of sensible objects of a deeper reality of which they are symbols

tions alike seem to presuppose. The necessity for immutable principles, if the world of nature and human life is to be explained, impressed itself upon Plato with all the greater force that he seems to have realized with peculiar vividness the mutability of much which ordinary experience pronounces permanent. To the element of reality which his mind discovered or surmised everywhere behind the appearance and change which sensation shows us, he gave the name of 'form'. It is a curious instance of the changes of fortune in the life of language, that the Greek word 'idea', which Plato chose to express what is most profoundly real, and least dependent on the human mind for its reality, should have come to be used for a mere mental creation or fiction, and that its English equivalent 'form' is now mainly suggestive of what is superficial and unsubstantial. The history of the word in Greek speculation before its employment by Plato is very slight; we can only conjecture that to a Greek, peculiarly organized for the perception of shape, and accustomed to find significant and typical lines in all that he saw, it was a natural transition from what is outwardly and visibly characteristic to what is inwardly and theoretically essential. Every people, like every individual thinker, has its favourite metaphors for expressing ultimate philosophical conceptions. In the phraseology of Greek philosophy there is no phenomenon of which we are more constantly reminded than that of vision, and the use of the word 'form' by Plato is only the most pregnant and far-reaching instance of a metaphor which, in

To this reality he gave the name of Form or Idea

the way of analogy, simile, or suggestion, pervades his speculation. We have here only to indicate in the briefest and most general way the meaning of the Platonic conception of 'form', so far as it enters into the theory of knowledge and education. It may be said to combine elements of all the modern conceptions of essence, law, and ideal. Those qualities or characteristics in a thing which most make it what it is, and which contrast with others that are casual and separable, are the 'form' which characterizes and individualizes the thing. That principle which gives consistency and continuity to changing manifestations of activity, is the 'form' which works itself out in a plastic material. And once more: the aim or mark to which the various steps in a process converge is the 'form' to which the agent in the process looks, and which he strives to attain. So that alike in art, in science, in morality, it is the 'form' which is essential and important, the 'form' which the imagination discerns through the chaos of sense-impressions, the 'form' which the reason separates from the accidental conditions of time and place, and the 'form' in which the moral consciousness finds rest and guidance amidst the distractions and contradictions of experience.

Plato has various ways of expressing the mode in which the 'form' exists, and is apprehended. It is that which really 'is', as opposed to that which 'seems'; that which is 'one', as opposed to that which is 'many'; that which is self-identical and permanent, as opposed to that which is always becoming some-

thing else. Or, again, the sensible world is only the
'appearance' of the intelligible; the things which we
see and hear are 'images', that only 'resemble' and
suggest something which we cannot see or hear; and
each of these images or resemblances only 'partici-
pates in', but does not adequately embody, the reality
which is grasped in and over it. The vivid and some- The
Reality
times crude manner in which Plato represents the which we
cannot see
relationship between what is and what is not 'form', or hear
has given rise to much misunderstanding of him as
well as to many real difficulties, and has left a doubt
whether he had himself clearly apprehended what
he was endeavouring to express. The truth seems to
be that no great genius, 'stung by the splendour of a
sudden thought', can ever work out or even conceive
his idea with the coolness and completeness which
are necessary to make it consistently intelligible and
to guard it from misinterpretation. But we are here
concerned, not with the exaggerations and confusions,
real or supposed, to which Plato fell a victim, but with
the central truth which he saw clearly, and to which
he held tenaciously.

Returning now to the scale of knowledge, we see
that whether we regard the sense of unsatisfactoriness
which impels the mind to advance upon sensible
opinion, or the intellectual condition in which that impulse results, it is what Plato understands by 'forms',
for which the mind is looking, and in which it
rests. The mathematical sciences, which spring from,
and are the answer to, questions raised by the mathematical properties of sensible objects, take account,

not of the particular figures to which they refer, but of the 'objects themselves', of which those figures are only the 'images'; these 'objects themselves' are clearly what we have learnt to know as 'forms'. Though, however, it is about the 'form' of the triangle or of unity that the geometrician and arithmetician really reason, not about the figures on the paper, they cannot dispense with those figures. They exercise intelligence, but intelligence which still has an appendage of sense, and is not therefore perfectly intelligent. And along with this imperfection in the knowledge of which mathematics are a type, goes another one which Plato expresses by saying that such knowledge is 'assumptive' or 'hypothetical'. 'Geometricians, arithmeticians, and the like, assume the odd, the even, the figures, the three kinds of angle, and other similar things, according to the particular branch of the science with which they are dealing; these they assume themselves to know, and make them hypotheses, and do not think themselves bound to give any further account of them either to themselves or others; they suppose every one to see the truth of them. From these hypotheses they start, and when they have got this start they go on through the remaining steps, and arrive conclusively at the result which was the original object of their inquiry.' Such a procedure does not satisfy the full conception of knowledge or science; for 'when the starting-point of the argument is something assumed and not known, and the end and intermediate steps depend for their connexion upon this unknown starting-point, how

[margin note: An example from mathematics.]

can such a conclusion possibly constitute knowledge?'
By 'hypotheses', then, Plato understands, not assumptions temporarily made for certain definite purposes, but truths which, while really depending for their validity upon their connexion with higher truths, are treated as if they were independent of that connexion, and self-proven. In this sense, each one of the 'forms' of existence with which the special sciences are concerned, number, figure, motion, &c., is a 'hypothesis'; and special sciences are scientific so far as they follow logically from these 'hypotheses' which form their principles, but so far as those principles themselves are not, strictly speaking, 'known', they do not satisfy the ideal requirements of science. For science to Plato means explanation and intelligibility; we 'know' a truth when we can 'give account of' it, and the way in which we give account of it is by showing its necessary connexion with wider and more independent truths. Progress in science is progress from isolated to connected thought; and if we try to imagine such a progress consummated, we are led to the conception of a universal science, in which every part The is seen in its relation to every other part, and of which vision of a universal the whole forms a perfect orb of truth, beginning and know- ledge, a ending in itself. Of such a science, as it might be if systematic unity of the speculative impulse of the human mind were fully truth. satisfied, Plato has given us a picture, though he is conscious that it is only a picture, and that to realize what he is imagining is 'a flight above' both himself and his readers. The whole matter of knowledge is imaged as a perfectly graduated scale of the essential

'forms' of existence; each 'form' is seen to be, not an ultimate truth, but a 'hypothesis', depending for its truth upon one above it; the mind mounts from 'form' to 'form', using each as a 'point of departure' to the next, until it reaches the topmost 'unhypothetical principle', upon which the whole chain hangs, and from which it can descend again securely down the ladder of intelligible reality. In such a perfect system of knowledge, as there would be nothing 'hypothetical' or unproven, so there would be no element of sense or unintelligibility. The symbolism of sensible appearances, which suggest imperfectly something which they are not, and blur the intellectual vision with an unexplained residuum, would melt into the perfect transparency of reason, when mind met mind face to face.

This is the fourth and last stage: knowledge

We have thus reached the highest stage in the Platonic scale of mental development, that stage to which he applies emphatically the name of 'knowledge', and the object-matter of which is the essential 'forms' of existence without admixture of hypothesis or sense. Like the preceding stage, it represents an inherent impulse in the mind; but, unlike it, it leaves the impulse in the main unfulfilled. The different specific sciences owe their existence to the dissatisfaction occasioned to the mind by reflection upon its sensible experience. The dissatisfaction they remove by revealing permanent and consistent 'forms' in what before seemed a fluctuating chaos; but it still survives in the sense of incompleteness and limitation which the mind feels, when it finds that each science

rests upon an unproven basis and points beyond itself
for the ultimate establishment of its conclusions. The
force or faculty in virtue of which the mind is per-
petually trying to rid itself of this dissatisfaction, to
get out of the region of 'hypotheses', and to see truth
as a whole of parts, is called by Plato the 'dialectical'
faculty, and the ideal science which the completed
exercise of that faculty might be conceived to create,
is the 'science of dialectic', the only form of science or
knowledge which seemed to him strictly to deserve
the name. The term 'dialectic', which plays almost
as conspicuous a part in the Platonic philosophy as
'form', means originally nothing more than the
process of oral discussion by question and answer.
Naturally a prominent and familiar word among
a people where ideas were communicated so much The
more by talking than by reading, and specially conse- science of
'Dialectic'
crated to Plato by the example of his master Socrates,
it was adopted by him to describe the process by
which the mind endeavours to arrive at true conceptions, whether by actual verbal discussion or by
inward 'dialogue with itself'. And as Plato conceived
that the truth exists in a certain form or order, and
that the human mind in learning and apprehending
it must conform to that order, he naturally used
'dialectic' for that particular mode of manipulating
language and thought which seemed to him most
consonant with truth, and most fitted to lead to its
discovery. What that mode must be we have already
had some indication. If the only conception of reality
which satisfied Plato was that of a cosmos which is

neither a vacant unity nor a crowded chaos, but a reasonable system of interrelated elements, the only true logic or method of knowledge must seem to him to be that which obeys the twofold requirement arising from such a conception, a method which unifies without confounding, which specifies without separating, a method which does not 'break the limbs' of truth, but follows and reveals the natural articulations of its subject-matter till it has reached the perception of its organic unity. Such a method is the true 'dialectic', the only true method of learning, teaching, and investigating, because the only method which is in agreement with the inherent constitution of the real world. And if the method be supposed to have been carried through to the utmost verge of truth, the moving process passes into a completed result, and dialectic, instead of a logic of discovery and definition, becomes the living expression of the truth itself, the embodied logic of reality. Plato has nowhere filled up the outline of his conception of 'dialectic'; but the greater part of his dialogues are practical illustrations of the principle, and the suggestions of a theory which are scattered up and down them are often more instructive as well as more stimulating than the finished systems of other men.

We have now seen how Plato conceived the natural order in the ascent of the mind towards truth. It begins by seeing things 'darkly', through the uncertain 'glass' of fancy; it goes on to the certainty of direct sensible experience; from the objects of sense and opinion, with their local and temporal limitations, it

The dwellers in the cave

advances to the perception of essential 'forms' and
principles, which those objects symbolize or suggest;
and from the understanding of isolated principles and
their consequences it passes to the apprehension of
them as steps in a connected scale of existence. We
have next to ask, How far does the human mind
actually obey this principle of progress? What is the
actual state and opinion of mankind as regards its
'education', in the fuller sense in which we have now
come to use the word? Plato has expressed his views
upon this subject in the famous allegory of the cave,
with which the seventh book of the *Republic* opens.
The allegory to be understood and appreciated
must be studied in its entirety. A few only of its
main features need be dwelt upon here. Mankind
in general, Plato gives us to understand, so far from
advancing up the road which leads to truth and light,
remain for the most part during their whole life in
the state of mind which is only fit for children. They
are like men sitting bound at the bottom of a cave,
lit by a fire to which their backs are turned, able only
to look straight before them at the wall of their prison.
The living world of nature and man lies behind them,
and all that they know of it are its shadows and echoes,
the hazy, unsubstantial, artificial reproductions of
the minds of other men. At this moving world of
phantasms they stare, and in its reality they believe,
with all the fixity and fervour of men who have done
a thing from their childhood. They watch its vain
shows as they pass and repass, observe the order of
their succession, and formulate a conjectural science

which is to enable them to predict the future. From this condition there is for most men no escape, for they do not know, and therefore cannot desire, any other sort of existence. Only now and then, by some force of nature or circumstances, a prisoner is set free from his chains, made to stand on his feet and look round, to see with his own eyes, and hear with his own ears, and step by step, perhaps, to make his way to the upper air and the sunlight of knowledge. But each stage in the process is grievous to him; the first experience of actual life confuses him, and makes him wish for his old world of fancy again, and the sudden revelation of scientific truth dazzles his mind, which is only used to empirical certitude. Only by slow degrees he gets an insight into the principles which really govern the world, and the supreme principle upon which they all depend; and if in compassion for the ignorance of mankind he tries to teach them his new knowledge, he is received with ridicule and opposition, which in the end may cost him his life.

Philosophy, like religion, has often begun by calling upon men to get rid of their prejudices and illusions. It is customary, indeed, to look upon the two as antagonistic, and to contrast the humility required by the Gospel with the supposed arrogance and self-sufficiency of the philosophic spirit. Yet if we take men so different, and so representative in their The right differences, as Plato, Bacon, and Spinoza, we find temper for philosophy them all agreeing, not in a glorification of the human and religion mind, but in the imperative demand that it should shake off its 'chains' and turn to receive the light, that it should surrender its 'idols' and 'become as a little child', that it should look at things 'under the form of eternity', not through the vague confusion of its own imagination. To all alike, however different their phraseology and their motive, the conviction is common, that there is an order of existence or of nature which man does not make but finds, which he must wait upon and not forestall, if he would attain to the well-being, the power, or the freedom, of which he is capable.

Passing from these common features to the details 'Shadows and of Plato's conception of human ignorance, we do not echoes' find him, like Bacon, giving any classification of the false 'shadows and images', but we can gather many hints as to their nature. Primarily they are the dim, exaggerated, and shallow representations of things through the medium of art, literature, and rhetoric. In explaining Plato's antipathy to dramatic representation, we have already had occasion to notice some of his attacks upon art in general. Those attacks seem to be valid if, and so far as, artistic representation produces actual illusion, and substitutes appearance for reality. To a mind which is really fitted by nature and education to receive art in the spirit of art, illusion, so far from being a necessary element in aesthetic enjoyment, is a distinct bar to it. A person who looks at a play exactly as if it were real life may be vehemently moved for a moment, but will eventually find the spectacle either so exciting or so wearisome that he will wish to interrupt it or to go away. It is essential to the perfect reception of artistic effect that the impulse to action should be in abeyance, and the theoretic faculties at their fullest activity. The after-effect may issue in acts, but at the moment of seeing, or hearing, or reading, the work of art, considered as such, demands that 'wise passiveness' which is only the other side of theoretic energy. But there are comparatively few imaginative persons in whom the double power of self-control and self-surrender, of created by entering in and yet of standing outside, is so strong art and literature that they 'cannot choose but' hear or see. To most of us the message of art awakens a cross echo in our own selves, and we go away with the flattering feeling that the vapours or the rhetoric of egoism are the universal types or tones of genius and truth. Then it is that the artist, often without knowing it, and against his will, becomes 'a mimic and a juggler' to the public; the spirit distilled in the crucible of imagination gets cloyed with the lees of prejudice or sentiment; and the 'impassioned expression, which is the counten-ance of all science', stiffens into a masquerade which can 'deceive children and fools'.

The 'shadows and echoes' amongst which Plato's prisoners live are not, however, only the illusions, intentional or unintentional, produced by art and literature; they are also the illusions of our own and by our passions. It would be a great mistake to regard the own passions darkness of the cave as a mere darkness of intellectual ignorance, or the escape from it as a mere intellectual enlightenment. In the mind of Plato, reason is never for long dissociated from emotion, or knowledge from purpose; the highest impulse to him is the impulse towards truth, and the highest knowledge is knowledge of the end of action. Thus the great reason why the spark of 'divine' intelligence is so nearly smothered in man is not primarily the difficulty of learning or the mysteriousness of nature; the fetters which bind the men in the cave are those 'leaden weights which the pleasures of gluttony and the like gather round them, and which turn the eye of the soul to the earth'. The 'impulse' which, if it had sway, would carry the soul out of the 'sea' of earthly life, to union with 'the divine, immortal, and eternal' to which it is 'akin', is checked and thwarted by no irresistible necessity or power of evil, but by the 'shells and stones and tangle' with which the 'delights of the table' gradually incrust it. The 'painted images of true pleasure', with which men choose to dwell, are the offspring of their own nature, which leads them about 'like cattle, with their heads down and eyes fixed upon their dinners, feeding and breeding, and kicking and butting one another because they cannot get enough'. It is not the thought of 'this unsubstantial pageant' which leads Plato, like Shakespeare, to call human life a 'dream'; rather it is the same feeling as that of Lucretius when he cries to man,

> 'Qui somno partem maiorem conteris aevi,
> Et vigilans stertis nec somnia cernere cessas.'

It is because men will not rouse themselves to the reality which is there if they had the eyes to see it, because they mistake the passing shows of sense for the eternal essence of which they are the mere outside, because they 'fight about shadows' of power and clutch after 'phantoms of good', that 'before they are well awake in this world they find themselves in the other, sleeping the heavy sleep of death'.

'How then' (and this is the third and last part of our question) 'are men to be led up to the light, as some are said to have gone up from Hades to dwell with the gods in heaven?' Or, as we may also put it (for it is upon progress in knowledge that the good of mankind depends), 'What kind of studies and practice will produce the men who are to save society?' Or, once more (for the interest of society is ultimately identical with that of its noblest natures), 'How is the commonwealth to handle philosophy so as not to be destroyed by it?' Clearly it is important that society should look to it; that her greatest sons, instead of being criminals or outcasts, who owe their mother nothing for their bringing up, should be bound to her by ties of mutual obligation. The principle of justice which regulates other spheres of life ought to hold good here too; the man who has the philosophic faculty should not be allowed to do what he likes with it; he should be induced to contribute his share to the common good, and to help in 'binding the commonwealth together', while his fellows should do for him what he cannot do for himself, provide him with the necessary material of life and supply his soul with the nurture which it demands. The general character, then, of the duty of society is clear: it has to find a way for doing methodically and with the greatest possible ease what now takes place exceptionally by the force of circumstances and under

How are men to be led up to the light?

almost insuperable obstacles. And the general character of the education which shall do this is also clear:
it must be an education which will help the soul to
'see' the truth, to penetrate the darkness which fancy
and appetite spread between it and facts, to follow its
own 'divine impulse', and to shake off the fetters of its
own forging. Some 'professors of education', indeed,
talk as if the soul were like a blind eye and teaching
were 'putting sight into it'. But the truth is that the
'eye of the soul', the 'organ with which it learns and
understands', is not like the eye of the body. The latter
is more or less independent of the rest of the organism,
and can be moved without it; but the former can only
be 'turned to the light' if the whole soul be turned with
it. The soul is not in pieces, but continuous; knowledge The eye of
in the highest sense is not an independent act of a part the soul
of the self, but that union of the whole with truth, in
which the lower parts are taken up into the higher
according to their capacities. It is not possible to be
habitually living the life of the lower elements, and
to keep the higher at their greatest efficiency. Evil
is the 'disease' of the soul, and to be or do evil and still
expect to exercise the highest psychical activity is as
reasonable as it would be, if body cured body by
contact, to expect the most diseased body to be the
best healer. It is from this point of view that Plato
denies the possibility of getting to know the real
nature of evil by personally experiencing it; the very
experience which is to be the object of knowledge
spoils the instrument by which it is to be known. The
'whole' soul then must be turned to the light, for the

'eye of the soul' is the highest element in it, and carries with it the other elements.

In another respect also the mental is unlike the bodily vision. The bodily eye may lose its power of sight and have it restored to it again, but the analogous faculty in the mind can neither be created nor destroyed; 'the other virtues of the soul, as they are called, seem to be nearly akin to those of the body, for they are not originally in existence, but are an after product of habit and practice; but the virtue of intelligence seems to belong to something altogether more divine, something which never loses its force, *turning to the light* but is made serviceable or unserviceable, helpful or harmful, according as it is turned to the light or not'. The power of mental insight still remains active in the warped soul of the clever scoundrel; it is the divine and immortal part of the soul, that which makes it 'capable of bearing all good things', but capable also of bearing 'all evil things'; it may be 'buried in the mud' of ignorance or overgrown with the 'incrustations' of passion, but it is never so lost that it cannot be lifted up, purged, and re-illumined, or so negative that anything else can be substituted for it.

The general principle, then, of the higher education *How can education bring about this 'conversion'?* is expressed in the term 'conversion'. How is this to be effected? Clearly the educational process must follow the true and natural order of mental development. If the scale of knowledge and truth is what it has been represented to be, education must be a method for leading the soul from the lowest stage, where it apprehends nothing but 'images', through that of direct sensible experience, to the region of essential 'forms' of existence, and so finally to that perception of the systematic unity of truth which is the ideal of science. The first two steps are provided for if the education in 'music' be successfully carried through. Its function was precisely to obviate the possible perversion of the imagination and emotions, by training them rightly; to prevent people from being still children when they ought to be men, by making childhood the real precursor of manhood; to train the imagination so that it should not lead to an idolatry of sensible forms which the mind can only leave with pain and difficulty, but that 'when reason comes' she may be 'welcome' to the soul which has already learnt to know her unconsciously; to form habits which may not be mere habits, but the basis for fresh acquisitions of character, and convictions which shall not be merely fixed, but shall offer a ready material for receiving the form of principles. In a soul thus trained, with its imagination filled with fair sights and sounds, its emotions instinctively responsive to what is really lovable, its beliefs 'dyed fast' with truth, the new structure of knowledge has to be reared. The steadfastness of opinion has to be translated into logical consistency; the quickness and exactness of perception and fancy into the power of abstraction and reasoning; the love of things and persons into the devotion to principles and ideas. What the first step in the new 'conversion' will be we already know by anticipation. The mathematical sciences, which are at once the product and the type of the third stage

The way has already been prepared in the elementary stage

in the scale of mental activity, are clearly marked out
to be the instruments for stimulating and training
that activity. Those sciences, as we saw, owe their
existence to the difficulties which the soul experiences
when it reflects upon the matter of sensuous opinion.
It is in meeting those difficulties, in obedience to
an inherent speculative impulse, that the soul passes
from the supposed clearness and consistency of local
and temporal truth to the more transparent clearness
and the more rigorous consistency of a truth which is
not sensible but intelligible. If, then, we could make
the soul perform methodically and under guidance
the process which it is its nature to perform imperfectly
and at random, if the sciences could be utilized
for training its scientific faculties as the arts were
utilized for training its artistic faculties, we should
be helping in the most effective, because the most
natural, way to 'make the work of conversion easy'.

Plato complains that the true educational function
of the sciences has been ignored or neglected. Arithmetic has been studied so far as is useful for trade and
commerce, geometry for the purposes of measurement, astronomy for its value in navigation, harmonics
in the interest of the professional musician; but it is
hard to make people believe the truth that each of
these sciences may be made a means for 'purging and
rekindling an organ of the soul which would otherwise
be spoiled and blinded, an organ more worth saving
than ten thousand eyes, for by it alone the truth is
seen'. He does not of course deny the importance of
such practical applications in their proper sphere;

on the contrary, he himself emphasizes the practical utility of arithmetic and geometry to a man who is to be a soldier and tactician. But he points out that for such practical purposes a very slight amount of science is necessary, and that the methods of study which serve for such purposes are not the methods which serve for education. The mere empirical observation of objects, which is all that is necessary for immediate utility, does not 'lead the soul to look upwards', whereas the study of the same objects in the scientific spirit is just what is wanted to make 'the natural intelligence useful instead of useless'. For, as we have already been told, the really scientific man, though he employs sensible objects in his reasoning, does not 'think of them'. The numbers of the arithmetician are such as 'can only be manipulated by thought'; and if we point out to him that the visible or tangible object which represents his unit is not 'one' at all, but is divisible into infinite multiplicity, he will only laugh at our simplicity, and will adhere to his assertion that one is one, and never anything else, invariable and indivisible. Geometry, too, so far as it is scientifically treated, relates to 'what is invisible and eternal', and not to the sensible figures which are 'becoming' something else at the very moment that we speak of them. Nor will Plato admit that the case is really different when we come to astronomy. Here indeed the splendour and beauty of the visible objects with which the science is concerned, easily deceive us into thinking that this merely sensible nature is in itself important and interesting. But

The true function of arithmetic, geometry, astronomy and harmonics

gazing up at the stars in open-mouthed wonderment will no more give us knowledge than gazing at a very excellently constructed diagram. The whole celestial universe, so far as it 'has body and is visible', is subject to the same conditions as other material things. It does not 'admit of knowledge' in the strict sense; it is a symbol, but not the truth symbolized. The material heavenly bodies, as such, do not realize the relations of figure and motion which they suggest; those relations 'cannot be apprehended by sight, but by thought only'; and it is as figures and diagrams for the discovery and analysis of these intelligible relations that the visible bodies ought to be used, if we are really to study astronomy and thereby to educate the human intelligence. The methods adopted in harmonics, or the science of sound, admit of a similar reform; it too may be made to help in the work of 'conversion' by revealing the abstract numerical conditions upon which musical harmony depends. But this is not understood either by the professional musicians who fight over the 'smallest audible interval' and 'set their ears before their minds', or even by the Pythagorean philosophers who, though they appreciate the true interest of the subject, confine their investigations to what they can hear, and do not go on to ask what relations of number produce harmony and what do not, and what is the cause of each.

Plato's conception, then, of the educational function of the sciences is, primarily, that they may be used to teach men to think. This they do by presenting to the mind sensible objects, and at the same time compelling it to ignore or abstract from the particularity and limitation incident to sense-presentation, to fix its attention solely upon the essential and universal 'forms' which are confusedly 'imaged' to sense, and to deduce consistently the consequences which follow from them. The difficulties or misunderstandings to which he has given occasion in expressing this conception, seem mainly due to the embarrassing combination of an extremely limited and simple scientific experience with an almost prophetic power of advancing upon it, or divining its possibilities. In the childlike confidence inspired by the still fresh perception of the nature of arithmetical and geometrical truth, he leaps the barrier which modern thought has erected between deductive and experimental science, and boldly surmises a state of human knowledge in which the whole web of cosmic conditions should be as rigorously intelligible as the simplest relations of number and figure. He sees how the senses confuse the reason in its early reflections upon units and triangles, and how the reason sets the senses at defiance and goes on its own way securely, and at a stroke he pictures to himself the whole phenomenal world seen as the symbol of an intelligible order. He knows by experience how the study of mathematics quickens the mind and compels the practice of abstract thinking, and there seems to him to be no reason why the whole of human science should not be pressed into the same high service, the education of the human race.

We have, however, mentioned only one, and the lesser one, of the motives which led Plato to advocate <sub-text>Not only to teach us how</sub-text>

to think, but to lead us to the knowledge of Reality the study of the sciences. The ten years between twenty and thirty, over which he would continue that study, would be a very long time to spend in the mere practice of logical thinking. But the study has to him a real as well as a formal significance. It serves not only as a mental gymnastic, helping the soul to reach the place where the truth is to be found, but also as an actual introduction to the truth for which it is looking. That this is Plato's conception appears both from his enumeration of the sciences themselves, and, still more, from the principle upon which he directs that they should be studied. In his series of sciences, arithmetic, geometry, stereometry, astronomy, and harmonics, he is clearly following an order of progression in their respective subject-matters— number, planes, cubes, motion of cubes, motion of audible bodies. We need not suppose the series to be intended to be complete, even in the then condition of knowledge; we are expressly told that there are many other forms of motion which might be mentioned; still it would seem that Plato meant to co-ordinate, in outline at least, those portions of the knowledge of his time which could pretend to the name of science. This appears more clearly from the passage in which he indicates the method upon which they should be studied. 'If the pursuit of all these subjects which we have enumerated be carried on to the point where they communicate with and are related to one another, and their natural affinities be inferred, I think it is of some use for our present purpose, and not labour spent in vain, as it otherwise is.' And again, when the age of twenty is reached, the branches of knowledge which have been placed before the student in boyhood 'promiscuously', to be picked up without system or constraint, ' are to be brought together, so that he may have a comprehensive view of their relationship to one another, and to the nature of being'. From these passages we see that Plato regarded the sciences which he had enumerated, not as arbitrary and isolated pieces of knowledge, still less as merely formal constructions, but as directly related to the sum of being or reality, of which each one of them expresses a particular aspect, and in which they all find a common meeting-point. Number, extension, motion, are primary 'forms' of being; the first especially is involved in the simplest acts of thought, and underlies the processes of all the arts and sciences. In learning to deal with them we are not only preparing ourselves for dealing with more important subjects, but we are actually setting our foot upon that 'ladder' of existence, the ascent of which would be the summit of scientific attainment. And here we are reminded of the language in which Plato explains what he considers to be the imperfection or inadequacy of the knowledge of which mathematics are a type. That knowledge, we were told, is 'hypothetical', that is, it rests upon principles which are unproven, because they have not yet been apprehended in all their relations to other principles. In requiring, then, that the study of the sciences should be constantly directed to the perception of their mutual relationships, Plato is clearly intending to remedy this characteristic defect by pointing the way from the region of the 'hypo-thetical' to that of a self-demonstrated system of knowledge. To such a system Plato, as we saw, gave the name of 'dialectic', and the impulse which leads, and the rules which guide, the mind in the endeavour to realize it, are the 'dialectical' faculty and method. Accordingly we find, as we might expect, that in the power of perceiving the mutual relationships of the particular sciences, Plato finds 'the greatest test of the presence or absence of a dialectical nature', for 'the man who can see things together is a dialectician, and he who cannot is not'. And as to 'see things together', or in their natural and necessary connexion, is the same thing as to understand, explain, or account for them, the 'dialectician' is also naturally described as the man who 'can give account both to himself and others of the essential nature of any given thing'.

to teach us to 'see things together'

The sciences, then, 'ordinarily so called', are the 'prelude' or the 'propaedeutic' to 'dialectical' science. The study of them, as usually conducted, is far from making a man a 'dialectician', for it generally leaves him incapable of 'giving any account of' his knowledge, and knowledge thus unaccounted for is neither an intelligent nor a permanent acquisition. But if studied on the principles above suggested, they not only 'purge and rekindle' the mental vision, they are not only 'fellow labourers in the work of conversion', but they also directly prepare the way for a higher study, partly by discovering and developing the requisite faculty for it, partly by introducing the mind to the elementary basis in that structure of knowledge of which 'dialectic' is 'the coping-stone'.

The study of the sciences during the ten years between twenty and thirty is not, in Plato's plan, to claim the whole time and energy of the citizen who is admitted to it. He is to be at the same time serving his apprenticeship in military service, and testing the courage of his moral convictions under the various trials of pleasure and pain, fear and persuasion, which meet him in the course of his public duties. The study of 'dialectic', on the other hand, which is to go on from thirty to about thirty-five, is to concentrate the entire faculties of the student while it lasts. Of the form and substance of this 'dialectical' science we can only collect hints from Plato. And, firstly, as to its form. If we conceive 'dialectic' as a body of scientific truth, it would be nothing less than a system of universal knowledge, in which not only the 'hypothetical' principles of the mathematical and physical sciences, but those of all other branches of human inquiry, found their place and justification, and were seen to depend upon a single 'unhypothetical principle'. Plato was as conscious as we are that no such universal science was in existence, but perhaps he felt more strongly than we do the importance of insisting upon its theoretical necessity, and of keeping the outlines of it before the mind. If, on the other hand, we think of the study of 'dialectic' as an educational study of the true method or logic of thinking, the simplest account of it is that it is 'that education which will enable the student to question and answer in the most scientific

'Dialectic' as the crown of the educational process

way'. This may seem to be a great fall from the height to which we are carried by the conception of a universal science, but this is mainly because we use oral discussion so comparatively little as a means for arriving at truth, and because our ideas of science and speculation are associated with printed books and systems, rather than with the living processes of thought which produce them. If we substitute for 'the man who can question and answer in the most scientific way', 'the man who can elicit, whether from his own mind or that of others, the truest thought on every subject which comes before him', we shall have a more adequate notion of what Plato meant. For if, as he conceived, truth is a system in which no part can be fully known until its connexion with all other parts has been apprehended, it follows that in proportion as a man can 'give and take account of' any subject, or part of a subject, he must have the system before his mind. We can therefore understand how Plato can say that 'no other procedure can undertake to give a complete and methodical grasp of the essential nature of any given thing'. For what is the case in what is commonly called discussion? Generally we go no farther with it than to produce a certain comfortable persuasion in our own minds or that of others; we appeal to no higher standard than the current opinions and desires of the public which we address; we are satisfied when we have turned a smart phrase or won a verbal victory. Even reasoning which aspires to be 'philosophical' is often only an artificial arrangement of skilfully adjusted words, which seem to have admirable coherence, but bear no relation to facts. But let us suppose a mind to which debate, whether outward or inward, has no other object than the attainment of truth; a mind bent upon arriving at and imparting conviction, and feeling that a lifetime is but a fragment in the eternity which such a work demands; suppose it filled with an insatiate desire for reality, which no fragment is so insignificant as *and its perfect work* to escape, no objections so formidable as to deter, no complexity so great as to confuse, no hypothesis so ultimate as to satisfy; suppose too that such a mind had been trained by many years' practice in the power of abstracting itself from the immediate presentations of time and place, so that it was able to 'let go eyes and other senses, and make its way to the real truth'; and suppose that there is present in it, not only the general desire for truth and the belief in the possibility of arriving at it, but also a conception, in outline only, but not therefore the less firm or definite, of the form in which the truth exists and in which it must be apprehended by the mind, a conception leading us to look everywhere for unity in multiplicity and differentiation in unity, so that while no piece of truth can be confounded with any other, no piece can be isolated from any other; and suppose, lastly, that this conception of the constitution of truth had borne fruit in an approximate systematization of the existing sum of knowledge, a logic of truth as complete as the state of the human mind at the time admits, and that this logic had been studied and practised unremittingly for years: then we shall perhaps have some idea of what Plato intended by the true 'dialectical' nature and the true 'dialectical' education.

We shall probably feel that such an education must The qualities of soul necessary to the study of it depend for its success more upon the spirit in which it is imparted and received than upon its particular form and matter. And certainly no one can be farther than Plato from the idea that 'dialectic' is a ready-made system of formulas to be swallowed whole by the mind. He is never tired of insisting upon the importance of choosing the right natures for the study of the sciences, and still more for that of 'dialectic'. They must be, not 'bastards', but 'genuine' children of philosophy; 'sound in limb and sound in mind', well grown and developed, not one-sided 'cripples'. They must not only be quick to learn, but must have also the qualities of intellectual retentiveness and endurance and love of work, 'for hard study makes a craven of the soul much more than gymnastic; the work comes more home to it, for the soul has it all to itself, and does not share it with the body'. Above all, they should be of the proper age, and should have been 'dyed' indelibly with the spirit of law and order, so that they may combine, what it is hard to find in combination, constancy and steadiness of character with speculative activity and aspiration. Otherwise the study of dialectic will continue to bring upon philosophy the charge which is so often made against it, that it unsettles the mind and undermines morality. For, as we have already heard, philosophy is a double-edged instrument; the speculative spirit which demands to have its beliefs justified and its experience accounted for, may by a turn of the hand become the spirit of revolution, denying the validity of all beliefs and the reasonableness of any experience; and the same logical method which, when rightly handled, guides us through the maze of opinion and reveals the essential forms of truth, may be applied by the intellectual gladiator to show that one thing is no more true than another, and to confound real distinctions in a mist of words. The danger lies in the transition from the atmosphere of 'opinion' to that of 'knowledge'. In the former we seem to be surrounded by a world of solid and permanent objects, each with a definite position and character of its own, with which our ideas are inseparably bound up. Our principles are materialized in particular persons and things, and these in their turn are invested with the sanctity of principles. Of the possible incongruity between an idea and its local and temporal embodiment we are as yet unconscious. But the mind has an inherent and a justifiable impulse to advance upon this state; for, as a matter of fact, truth is not merely local or temporal, and however necessary it may be that our experience of it should be so, it will be continually, so to say, giving the lie to that experience and breaking the limitations imposed upon it. And in this capacity which the mind possesses of rising above itself, asking itself questions, feeling dissatisfaction with its own results, lies the real condition and source of progress, intellectual and moral. But the difficulty is to regulate the capacity rightly, to awaken it at the right moment, and to exercise it in the right method. The power of logical manipulation in clever people is often far in advance of the strength of their character. The first sense of command over logical formulas, not unlike that of command over literary expression, is apt to upset the balance of the mind, which feels as if it had the world at its command, because it can set it up and knock it down again in syllogisms. Many of us must have observed, as Plato had done, 'that schoolboys, when they get their first taste of logic, make free with it as if it were a game; they are for ever using it to contradict people, and in imitation of those who confute them they go and confute others, as pleased as puppies to worry and tear every one who comes in their way'. But there is a more serious danger than that arising from the mere delight in the exercise of a new accomplishment. The 'flattering' voice of pleasure is always encouraging the intellect to find a flaw in the beliefs and institutions in which we have been brought up. The 'questioning spirit' comes to us and asks 'What is honour?' 'What is justice?' We answer by pointing to this and that belief, this and that course of action, according to what we have been taught. But logic has no difficulty in confuting us, in showing that this particular belief or action is in itself 'no more right than wrong'; for the particularity of the belief or the act is just what is unessential to their moral quality, as the particular colour or size is unessential to the mathematical quality of a triangle. It is only as 'partaking in' or 'imaging' something which cannot be apprehended in the limits of sensible experience, that the particular phenomenon has a moral value. But if the mind has not yet realized this, if it has only realized the relativity of the particu- lar form of presentation, it will probably identify the unessential and phenomenal conditions with this essential reality, and in ceasing to believe in them will cease to believe in anything at all. Against such a tragic result, which brings discredit on philosophy and turns into enemies of society men capable of being its saviours, Plato would guard by putting off real philo- sophical study till thirty, restricting it as far as possible to those characters which combine the requisite moral constancy with the requisite speculative interest and ability, and preparing for it by a long and severe discipline both in intellectual and practical work. In other words, he would not have 'the question' asked until the mind is already on the way to answer it, or the 'reason why' given until it merely means the throwing of a stronger light upon truth already seen. 'Dialectic' should 'destroy hypotheses', but only 'in order to establish them'; it should lead the mind to see through empirical facts, but not into a darkness or vacuum, only a wider vista of clearer truth.

A systematic study of philosophy, in the spirit and under the conditions suggested by Plato, is as remote from the modern theory and practice of education as a systematic employment of the arts. His account of what actually took place in his time might be applied with slight modifications to our own: 'Those who study philosophy at all, do it in this way: when they are just emerged from boyhood, in the intervals of business and money-making, they go into the most difficult part of the subject, I mean logic, and then they leave it; I am speaking of those who become the greatest proficients; and in after years if they ever accept an invitation to listen to a philosophical discussion, they are quite proud of themselves, for they look upon it as a mere pastime; and as they draw towards old age, their light goes out, all but that of a very few, and is never kindled again.' Philosophy in modern England has not even the advantage, a dubious advantage perhaps, of that conventional glory which attached to the word in the society of Plato's day, when a 'philosopher' seems to have combined in himself the lofty associations of the 'savant' with the social prestige of the 'man of culture'. It would hardly now be said of philosophy that it is 'a place full of fair names and shows', into which the 'escaped convicts' of other professions 'are glad to take a leap'. In the popular estimation it is a cold and comfortless region, haunted mainly by the fancies of dreamers, the sneers of sceptics, and the formulas of pedants. Not, indeed, that it is looked upon with less suspicion on that account. The cry is as loud now as it was in Plato's time, that speculation unsettles and corrupts the mind of the young. And if we may retort with him that the so-called theories upon which society is so hard are often nothing but its own opinions articulately expressed, and though we may not attach so much importance as he did to the love of speculative truth and the dangers of its perversion, we cannot deny that the forcible or adroit expression of what many men are dumbly feeling has in itself an incalculable power, and that not only are many honest minds needlessly perplexed by speculative writing and discussion, but that much real force of intellect and character is spoiled or frittered away by the want of method and management in the higher branches of our education. But though we may still feel the reality and presence of Plato's difficulties, we are as far as he could be from any prospect of applying his remedies. If the idea of concentrating the efforts of literary and artistic genius upon education seemed chimerical, what are we to think of the proposal that our best and ablest men should combine a severe course of scientific study with the first ten years of active life, and then give exclusive attention to logic and metaphysics for five years more? Or, even if the proposal itself were more likely to find favour or attention, where is that co-ordination of the sciences, and, still more, where is that science of logic, which could, with any confidence, be set before an aspiring mind? In the case of this, as of others of the most valuable ideas in the *Republic*, we are reduced to content ourselves with the crumbs which fall from the 'feast of reason'. In the way of its literal execution we can do hardly anything; but we might do a little towards carrying out some of its spirit. We might introduce more continuity into the curriculum of our schools and universities, trying to give the mind its natural food at the right times, and not letting it be still sprawling on the ground when it ought to be able to walk, nor asking it to climb a mountain before it can find its way about the house. The writers and supporters of our periodical literature might have more sense of the responsibility of their calling, and realize more fully that they spread truth or falsehood, as well as provide excitement or relaxation. Above all, we might convince ourselves that speculation, when it deserves the name, does not mean spinning cobwebs or playing with fireworks, but the finding of clews in the chaos of fact, and the letting in the daylight through the mist of prejudice; and that the speculative spirit, though it may have many counterfeits, is a real element in human nature, and an element to which it owes both its most splendid achievements and its most disastrous failures. To discuss the details of any educational system, actual or possible, would be far beyond the scope of an essay, and would be especially fruitless when the position of the natural sciences in education and their relation to philosophy is still a subject of so much dispute. As long as the advocates of scientific education suppose themselves, or are supposed, to be in essential antagonism to those of a literary education, and as long as metaphysics is understood to mean a mass of exploded fancies, there can be no common ground between ourselves and Plato. His whole theory hangs upon the principle that the study of the sciences should be complementary to a previous training through literature and art, and should itself be supplemented in turn by a study of those universal logical principles to which it points, and in which its problems find solution. Amongst ourselves the educational use of science, apart from its teaching for practical application, can only be said to have just begun, and is still mostly confined to the popularization of certain elementary truths with a view of stimulating early habits of observation and an interest in external nature. The idea of a systematic exhibition of the leading principles of the sciences, such as should not only train the mind to think, but should awaken its perception of the real nature of the world in which it lives, and 'draw it gently out of the outlandish slough' in which it is half buried, is still only an idea. Nor can the existing teaching of philosophy be said to satisfy Plato's requirements any better than that of science. A not very profound knowledge of small portions of Plato and Aristotle, a smattering of the history of philosophy mainly derived from second-rate handbooks, or a familiarity with some generalized theory of evolution, represent the chief part of what we can point to as the results in this branch of education. Meantime the air teems with speculation and discussion; questions are raised and answered in newspapers and periodicals which could hardly have been printed twenty years ago without raising an uproar; and there is no lack of those 'young men of talent, able to skim the surface of everything that is said, and to draw inferences from it as to the best way of leading their lives', of whom Plato anxiously asked, 'What are we to suppose that they will do?' In the dearth of really original contemporary speculation, we seem to be driven back upon a work only less difficult than that of creation, the work of interpreting the past. The task of editing philosophical books for educational purposes requires, as much as any task, real editorial genius, and as yet it has scarcely been attempted; nor have we any adequate collection of the most valuable parts of great philosophical writings, such as can be put into the hand of students. Perhaps, if the present interest in elementary education is ever followed by an equal interest in its higher grades, the expenditure of industry and ability upon primers and handbooks will be paralleled by an effort to make accessible to the more advanced minds of the community some of the original works which are now being made meat for the babes. We cannot expect to revive the days when truth was communicated by question and answer, though we may adopt some of their method on a humble scale; but it is all the more important that the few men in each generation who might once have discussed philosophy in the streets of Athens or the gardens of the Academy should make the works of the great thinkers of the world not a dead letter, but a living voice, by entering into their spirit, interpreting their speech, and carrying on their thought.

We have been thus far considering the Platonic education in science and 'dialectic' mainly in its

The purpose and the end formal aspect, and we have found in it a method for leading the soul from the stage in which its knowledge is held in the form of opinion and imagination to that in which it is held in the form of an intelligible system. But we have heard scarcely anything of the matter or substance of the education: much about the way in which it is to teach the mind to think, little of *what* it is to teach. And the question which now remains to be asked, and the answer to which puts the coping-stone to Plato's theory of education, is, What is the ultimate lesson which the human mind has got to learn, and for the sake of which all this elaborate apparatus has been put together? In the language of Plato's allegory, Where is the upper air to which the prisoners have to ascend, and what is the sun to which their eyes have to be turned? Or, in his technical phraseology, What is that unhypothetical first principle upon which the whole structure of truth depends, and to grasp which is the crowning act of knowledge? We have already seen briefly and by anticipation what is Plato's answer to these questions. It is 'the form of the good' which is 'the greatest of all studies'; it is this which 'comes last in the world of knowledge'; it is this which is the end of the 'dialectical' process, the ultimate principle to which all the 'hypotheses' of knowledge are to be referred.

The word 'good' has so many meanings and associations in English, that it is important to be clear as to the particular sense in which its Greek equivalent was used by Plato. That sense is perhaps most simply and most clearly illustrated in the familiar expressions, 'What is the good of a thing?' and 'What is a thing good for'? The answers to both these questions will give us the use, purpose, or end, which the thing in question serves, and when we say a given thing is 'good' in this sense, we can generally paraphrase the expression into 'it does its work, or serves its purpose, well'. From this sense is to be distinguished what would commonly be called the more 'moral' sense of 'good'. It is indeed difficult to say how far the two uses have

'The For: of the Good'

modified one another; but in the minds of most people there is a tolerably marked distinction between the sense in which they speak of 'a good man' and that in which they speak of 'a good horse' or 'a good plough'. In the former case they think primarily of a certain state of mind or character, secondarily of the end which it fulfils, or the work in which it is manifested; in the latter, the work which the horse or plough does is the first consideration, the conditions of their doing it come second. We shall understand, not only Plato, but the whole Greek moral philosophy, better, if we bear the second use of 'good' in mind; if we accustom ourselves to think of man as having a specific work to do, of morality as his doing that work well, of virtue or 'goodness' as the quality which makes him do it well, and of 'the good' as that which the work serves or realizes, and in serving and realizing which it is itself 'good'. Unfortunately the modern associations with the word 'good' in this sense are somewhat narrow and misleading. When we ask, What is the 'good' of a thing? we are apt to think of the 'good' in question as a purpose or end outside the thing itself, to which it is made or supposed (perhaps only by ourselves) to contribute; and it is to this perversion of a true idea that the doctrine of final causes owes much of its deserved disrepute. To conceive of a thing as good for something, or having some good, is, in the truest sense of the words, nothing more than than to conceive of it as having a meaning or being intelligible; for, strictly speaking, a thing of which the elements exist side by side in no connexion or order

What is meant by 'the Good'?

whatever, or a thing which itself exists by the side of other things without standing in any expressible relation to them, is to our intelligence an inconceivable nonentity. And the moment that we mentally interpret a thing, or, in other words, understand it, we give it a reason for existing, whether that reason be a form which it assumes, a purpose which it serves, a function which it performs, or a substance which it is. We may protest as vigorously as we can against the utilitarian or pietistic applications of such a conception; we may warn students of science against the dangerous tendency to anticipate nature, and to translate facts into the formulas of their own wish or fancy; but such protests and warnings touch only the abuse, not the essence, of the conception, that the world is not an unmeaning chaos, but a something of which, however slowly and with however many mistakes, we are discovering, and not merely inventing the significance.

It seemed necessary to make these few preliminary remarks in order to get a point of departure for considering Plato's account of 'the good' in the *Republic*. That account may be treated conveniently under three heads, according as 'the good' is regarded from an ethical, a logical, or a metaphysical and religious point of view. And firstly, 'the good' is 'that which every soul pursues, and for the sake of which it does all that it does'; it is the object in life which all men more or less feel themselves to have, but which very few clearly conceive or could clearly express; it is that which makes everything which we do seem worth doing, and everything which we possess worth possessing; that about which no one would willingly deceive himself, but of which every one says or thinks, 'this at least is something real, and this is what I really live for'. Theories of life apparently the most opposite imply the existence of this conception; the man who lives for pleasure does not really live for pleasure pure and simple; he admits the distinction of 'good' and 'bad' pleasures, and he chooses the good ones, in other words, those which fall in with his general scheme of life, however fragmentary or dim that scheme may be. So, too, with those who live for knowledge; it is not mere intellectual insight which is their aim, but insight into something 'good', something which they think worth knowing or having; for what is all knowledge worth unless it have some relation to our life, unless it show us what is the good in our life, and in the world where it is lived? And yet, though every one has, more or less consciously, some such ultimate object, something about which he would wish to be sure, something which makes things worth doing and having, it is here more than in any other point that the ignorance of mankind is most conspicuous. Most people 'have no one mark in life at which to aim in all that they do', and are more sure about anything almost than about the real object of their desire. The immediate steps which they take, the present means which they employ, seem to them much more clear than the ultimate goal to which they aspire. And this uncertainty of aim reacts upon the rest of their life; the proximate advan-

tages which they grasp at elude them and turn out
profitless, just because they have no connexion, no
pervading purpose, no whole in which they find a
place. It is the same want of unity and consistency ^{An intelli-}
which makes most of our moral ideas and character ^{gible stan-}
so vague and insecure. We talk of our principles of ^{value}
justice and honour, but how can we be said to understand, or even to possess, a principle or a virtue, unless
we see 'wherein they are good', unless we know what
it is which gives them their value, unless they are not
isolated fragments in a vague 'sketch' of life, but
connected parts in a fully wrought design? How can
a man order his own life or that of others, if he has
'no clear pattern in his soul' to the ideal truth of which
he can look for guidance? How can he maintain
existing laws or institutions, or reform them when
they need it, if his acquaintance with them is the merely
empirical familiarity which a blind man might have
with things he had often touched, or with a road along
which he had learnt to walk straight? Such a man
is only half awake; the good things which he supposes
himself to secure are only images and shadows of the
truth; his mental grasp of them is conventional and
unintelligent, and is liable to be loosened by every
logical objection. He can 'give no account' of them
to himself or others, can see no single 'form' underlying
their variety, but confuses what is essential in them
with what is unessential, the fragment with the whole,
the resemblance with the reality.

It is the perception of 'the good', then, which is
required to complete morality, to do away with the

vagueness, the aimlessness, the blindness, the frag-
mentariness, of life, and to give it unity, completeness,
and decision. But Plato sees in it the condition, not
only of conduct, but of knowledge also. What the
sun is in the world of visible objects, that he conceived 'the good' to be in the sphere of intelligence.
To the complete fact of sight there are, in Plato's view,
four factors necessary, an eye capable of seeing, an
object capable of being seen, light in the eye and the
object, and the sun of which the light is an 'effluence'.
The fact of knowledge may be analogously analysed:
there must be a subject capable of knowing and an
object capable of being known, there must be intelligence present in both making the one intelligent and
the other intelligible, and there must be a source of
intelligence from which it is diffused through the
twin world of subject and object, soul and being.
Such a source is 'the good', which 'supplies truth to
the object of knowledge, and gives to the subject the
power of knowing'. Nor is this all: as the sun is the
condition not only of vision and visibility, but also
of birth, growth, and nurture to visible things, so the
objects of knowledge owe to 'the good', not only their
truth, but also their very being and essence. And
lastly, like the sun in the allegory of the cave, 'the
good' is the crowning vision in the upward progress
of the soul from darkness to light; or, speaking without
metaphor, if the soul, in the strength of the dialectical
impulse, penetrates right through the imagery of
sense, and traverses the whole chain of intelligible
relations, the 'end of the intelligible' at which it

(marginal note) A 'sun' in the sphere of intelligence; the working out of this idea

arrives, the 'unhypothetical first principle', upon which it sees the whole structure of knowledge to depend, is again 'the good'. In Plato's mind then, the conception of knowledge and truth, the conception of objective reality or essence, and the conception of a systematic order or cosmos, alike implied the conception of a 'good', which cannot be identified with any of them, but is the condition or logical *prius* of them all. Things are known and understood so far as they are seen as elements in a rational order; knowledge is the perception of them as such, and things so perceived are truly perceived. Again, a thing is what it is in virtue of its position in such an order. As in the physical organism the character of each organ depends upon its relation to the whole, and has no existence apart from that relation; as in the larger whole of the state each member only preserves his true individuality so long as he takes his proper place in the organization of labour, and loses it when he ceases to do so; so in the universal order of existence, each constituent not only is understood, but subsists, only so far as it remains true to its place in the order, and as that place is determined by the ruling principle, end, or 'good', of the order, it is to this ultimately that it owes what it is. Lastly, as a life without purpose is blind, as qualities without unity and connexion are sketchy and incomplete, so a system of truth without an unconditioned principle to depend on is baseless and 'dreamy'; and such an unconditioned principle Plato could only conceive in the form of an absolute end which casts a light

The Ruling Principle in the order of the universe determining the position of each part

backward through the whole system of existence, but
The Ab- is itself above and beyond it. It thus becomes intelli-
solute End gible how he could speak of sciences so abstract as the
mathematical as leading up to 'the good', of geometry
as 'making us see the form of the good more easily',
and of the study of harmony as 'useful for the investi-
gation of the beautiful and good'. For, if each science
deals with a particular 'form' of universal being, and
each 'form' points to and connects with the 'form'
above it, and ultimately the highest 'form', then even
in the simple relations of number, figure, and sound,
we may expect to hear the faint 'prelude' to the far-off
'strain' of that fuller intelligence 'whose voice is the
harmony of the world'.

From this conception of a logically implied con-
The dition or postulate of the world of knowledge, it was
Creative
Cause to Plato an easy step to the conception of a creative
cause of the universe, both material and intelligible,
and we are not surprised to hear the sun spoken of,
not only as the 'analogue', but as the 'begotten child',
of the good. Plato seems here to have combined
the metaphysical conception which he expresses in
the *Phaedo* with the more mythological ideas of the
Timaeus. In the former dialogue the 'choice of the
good and the best' is represented as the essential
characteristic of intelligence, and any one who holds
that the universe is really the work of intelligence is
bound to show that 'it is the good and right which
binds and holds it together'; for it is folly to think that
we shall ever find 'an Atlas' to support it 'more mighty
and more immortal and more sustaining' than this.

In the *Timaeus*, 'the maker and father of the universe', whom 'it is hard to find out and impossible to declare to every one', being himself good, and therefore incapable of envy, creates the sensible world in all things as good, that is as like himself, as the conditions of sensible existence allow. The whole material universe is thus the 'image' or expression to sense of an intelligible system, and though this intelligible system is sometimes spoken of as the 'pattern' upon which the Creator made the world, it seems to be practically absorbed in the Creator himself when, at the end of the work, the visible cosmos is said to be 'the image of its maker, God manifest to sense'. In the light of these passages we may interpret the account of the good in the *Republic*. It is the final cause of the world; not that

'far-off divine event,
To which the whole creation moves',

but the immanent reason in things, in virtue of which each realizes its own end in realizing that of the whole. It is also the eternally creative power which sustains existence; which imagination represents in 'picture-language' as a person making all things good, and which reason apprehends as the 'unhypothetical principle' which all truth and goodness lead up to and imply. Art, morality, and science have each something to tell of it, for it is 'in a manner the cause of all that we know', whether in a more or a less perfect form. It is foreshadowed in the child's story of the God who is perfectly good and unchangeable, in the poem which presents the 'image of the good

The Immanent Reason in things

character' in its simplicity and integrity, in the beauty of line and melody which speak of 'that beauty in which all things work and move'. Or again, it is the divine beneficence which does no evil, the moral perfection in which our fragmentary virtues find their 'filling up', the spirit of a world where injustice is neither done nor suffered, and which we may look at until we become like it. Or, once more, the sciences put us on the ascent which leads to it, and surrender their hypotheses to receive them from it again connected and established; philosophy teaches us to find the outlines and articulations of its presence under the motley confusion of appearances; and the working life of mature and educated manhood supplies the rough material in which those who have mastered their lesson in theory may learn to understand and work it out in practice. For we must not forget that the fifteen years of training in sciences and dialectic are to be followed, in Plato's scheme, by fifteen more years of public service, 'in order that the citizen may not be behind the rest in experience'; and during all this time he is to be tested in the strength of his mind and character, 'whether he will stand being pulled about this way and that, or will blench at all'. Not till he has 'passed through this trial and shown himself foremost both in action and in knowledge', is he to be made 'to turn the eye of his soul upward and look at the very good itself, which is the universal source of light'. Then at last the world will lie open before his mind, ordered and intelligible, connected and pervaded by a single principle which he can trace in

many forms and combinations, but can distinguish The Whole
from them all. Then the shadows and images of ^of Truth
everyday life will acquire their true meaning, for he
will see through and over them to the realities which
they reflect. The isolated and self-contradictory
maxims of popular morality will interpret themselves
into fragments of a single perfection, which human
life suggests though it does not realize it. The separate
sciences will cease to talk 'in dreams', and will point
beyond themselves to the waking vision of an absolute
being. Philosophy will be, not a cunning device of
words or an occupation for a listless hour, but the
articulate language of truth which a lifetime is too
short for learning. Only eternity can interpret that
language fully, but to understand it is the nearest
approach to heaven upon earth, and to study it is
true education.